Library and Information Service

Library materials must be returned on or before the last date stamped or fines will be charged at the current rate. Items can be renewed online, by telephone, letter or personal call unless required by another borrower. For hours of opening and charges see notices displayed in libraries.

D1461076

A 8029 01 559791

Competitors run up the hill into Farndon during the MBNA Chester Marathon.

CROWOOD SPORTS GUIDES
MARATHON
AND HALF-MARATHON RUNNING
SKILLS · TECHNIQUES · TRAINING

Steve Trew

THE CROWOOD PRESS

First published in 2012 by
The Crowood Press Ltd
Ramsbury, Marlborough
Wiltshire SN8 2HR

www.crowood.com

British Library Cataloguing-in-Publication Data
A catalogue record for this book is available from the British Library.

ISBN 978 1 84797 338 2

Dedication
As ever, for Shane and Marilyn

Acknowledgements
My grateful thanks to Kath Atkin and Phil Pearson for their massive input to diet and nutrition, injury prevention, flexibility and strength training.

Photographs © Nigel Farrow

Typeset by Bookcraft Ltd, Stroud, Gloucestershire
Printed and bound in Singapore by Craft Print International Ltd

CONTENTS

PART I
INTRODUCTION TO MARATHON RUNNING

CHAPTER I

HISTORY AND MYTHS

Ancient History or Myth?

The first Persian invasion of Greece took place in 490BC. Vastly outnumbered, a force of 10,000 citizen-soldiers, mainly Athenians, engaged the invaders on the plain of Marathon to the north of Athens and won a decisive battle. The casualties were recorded as 192 Athenians, 11 Plataea soldiers and 6,400 Persians. The Athenians rightly regarded this victory as a decisive moment in their history and it marks the rise of Athenian democracy.

Before setting out from Athens for Marathon, the generals sent a herald off to Sparta to request their help. The herald's name was Pheidippides, a trained runner. According to the Greek historian Herodotus, he reached Sparta on the very next day after quitting the city of Athens – the direct distance is estimated at 135–140 miles. Having delivered the generals' request, he then returned to Athens with the Spartans' reply that, due to religious observances, they could not leave Sparta until the full moon. When they received this news, the Athenian generals decided to attack the Persians anyway.

A further feat of endurance took place after the battle when the Athenians were alerted to a Persian fleet sailing for Athens. Having fought in battle, and still wearing their armour, they set off back to defend Athens and arrived before the Persians – a distance of 26 miles.

The Start of the Modern Olympic Games

Almost twenty-four centuries later, in 1896, the first modern Olympic Games were held in Athens, Greece. The French historian Michele Breal proposed re-enacting the legendary marathon in an event that would test the athletes' powers of endurance; he also offered to put up a silver trophy for the winner. Baron Pierre de Coubertin, the inspirer of the modern Olympic Games, and Dimitris Vikelas, the Greek scholar who was also the first president of the International Olympic Committee (IOC) from 1894 to 1896, took the idea on board with great enthusiasm. The legend of the Marathon victory was therefore honoured by a 40km (25 mile) run from the Marathon bridge to the Marble Olympic Stadium of Athens.

Athens, Greece

The host nation of the first Olympics became ecstatic as Spyridon Louis, a Greek water-carrier, won the final, climactic race on 10 April in 2h, 58min, 50sec. 'The Marathon' was born. Spyridon Louis, as the first Olympic Marathon gold medallist, became a legend, and the course from Marathon to Athens, used today for the annual Athens Classic Marathon, became known as the 'authentic' or the 'original' marathon course.

The next two Olympic Marathons were run over similar distances, being hosted in Paris in 1900 and St Louis in 1904. A Parisian, Michel Théato, won the marathon in Paris after much controversy, whilst Thomas Hicks, a Briton running for the USA, won the St Louis Olympic Marathon under even more bizarre circumstances.

Paris, France

There were persistent rumours that the Paris marathon winner, Michel Théato, took a short-cut through the Paris back-streets. The Olympic historians André Drevin and Raymond Pointu exonerated Théato, but nobody was really sure what actually happened such a long time ago. Another point of interest in the Michel Théato saga is that he was a Luxembourg national, a fact that was not registered at the time. It emphasizes how disorganized the Olympic organization was in those days.

St Louis, USA

Even stranger things were to happen at the marathon at the St Louis 1904 Olympic Games, which was held in 90°F with only one drinks station, a 'water well' at the 12-mile (19km) mark. It was hardly surprising that only 14 of 32 starters finished the marathon. The 40km (25-mile) course started with five laps around the stadium track. The runners then left the stadium and started on a dusty, unpaved course that took them up-and-down over seven different hills. The path was marked by red flags that showed the route, while horsemen cleared the trail along the way. They were followed by doctors, judges and reporters in cars (only just invented!). Only after this procession were the marathon runners to be seen! The net result was a constant cloud of dust kicked up into the runners' faces. The first man to cross the finish line was Fred Lorz from New York City. Lorz completed the race in just over 3h. However, Lorz's victory did not last very long. Just as Lorz was about to accept his medal, it was discovered that he had accepted a lift in a car! It seems that Lorz had been suffering from stomach cramps, so he accepted the lift at the 9-mile (14.5km) point. He then rode in the vehicle for another 11 miles

(18km), at which point the car overheated and broke down. Lorz, now totally rested and recovered, rejoined the race. He later claimed that he never meant to cheat and was going to tell everyone what he had done. Lorz was immediately banned for life from any future amateur competition. (This ban was lifted a year later and Lorz went on to win the Boston Marathon in 2h, 38min, 25sec).

It was a British-born man named Thomas Hicks, representing the USA, who actually won the marathon in a time of 3h, 28min, 53sec. When he ran into the stadium, the crowd barely noticed him! They had already welcomed home the original (cheating) winner.

Immediately after the finish, Hicks had to be carried off of the track. At the 10-mile (16km) point he had been given an oral dose of strychnine sulphate mixed into raw egg white to keep him going. This was followed by further doses and also brandy. At the end of the race, Hicks had to be supported by two of his trainers so that he could cross the finish line; he almost died.

There were still more bizarre occurrences with another entrant, Cuban postman Felix Carvajal. Felix set about raising money for his travel to St Louis; one method he used was to run around the central square in Havana and then to jump on to a soapbox pleading for donations. He did this again and again and again until he raised the necessary cash.

On his way to the race, Felix managed to lose all of his money gambling in New Orleans and ended up hitchhiking his way to the Olympic Games (not that easy in 1904). When Carvajal arrived at the games, he had no running clothes and the marathon start was postponed while he cut the sleeves off his shirt and the legs off his trousers. He ran the marathon in

ordinary (but fairly light) shoes. During the race, Felix was extremely relaxed, talking to the spectators and even running backwards at times.

And then Felix got hungry. First he ate some peaches that he had stolen from a race official, and then he stole and ate some green apples. Not surprisingly he developed stomach cramps and had to drop out. However Felix eventually decided to continue and finished in fourth place. He probably would have won if he had not eaten all that fruit.

London, England

Finally, the marathon came of age at the 1908 Olympics in London, where the marathon was to find its now standard distance of 26 miles, 385yd (42.195km). The distance originally planned for was again 25 miles (just short of 40km), but the route from the start at Windsor Castle (designed and selected to win royal patronage) to the newly built stadium at White City was closer to 26 miles (41.842km) and the course manager fixed this as the distance from the start to the stadium entrance.

Another team was responsible for what happened inside the stadium, and the distance from the entrance to the finish line in front of the royal box was 385yd (352m). This was in a clockwise direction around the 536.4m track (one-third of a mile), at a time when races would be run either way around the track. If they had chosen to run the track the other way around, the distance would have been about 160m less, changing the classic marathon distance forever.

The winner was the American runner, Johnny Hayes, although the Italian athlete, Dorando Pietri, entered the stadium first

and then collapsed five times as he staggered around the track. He was later, on appeal from the Americans, deemed to have been 'assisted' by officials over the final 30m, and disqualified. Due to the resulting controversy, he was awarded a gold trophy by Queen Alexandra for his efforts.

Of far greater significance for the marathon was that the furore had piqued the interest of the betting community and a series of re-matches was set up in the following year, mainly in the United States, over courses of exactly the same distance. It was this first 'marathon boom' following on from the 1908 Olympics that eventually led to the distance being officially adopted at the 1924 Paris Olympics.

The Evolution of the Half-Marathon

The half-marathon as a racing distance gradually became more popular, as runners saw it as an intermediate step from racing 6 miles/10,000m before going on to the full marathon. At the BUPA Great North Run Half-Marathon last year, there were over 54,000 competitors! In 2000, The Copenhagen/Malmo Half-Marathon had almost 80,000 finishers.

The half-marathon is, of course, a very challenging distance to complete, but doesn't require quite the same amount of preparation as a full marathon. A half-marathon race will often be held in conjunction with a full marathon over some of the full-marathon course. For 'new' marathoners reading this book, it is strongly suggested that competing in a half-marathon should be seen as a prerequisite before racing a full marathon. The suggested training schedules will reflect this.

CHAPTER 2

THE BIG RACES (AND THE SMALL ONES)

The London Marathon

The running boom really started in America in the 1970s, and in Great Britain just a little later in 1981. The impetus for the surge of runners? The London Marathon. British Olympians Chris Brasher and John Disley had entered and run in the 1979 New York City Marathon. When they returned after the event, Brasher wrote an article, 'The World's Most Human Race'. In part he wrote:

> ... you must believe that the human race can be one joyous family, working together, laughing together, achieving the impossible. Last Sunday, in one of the most trouble-stricken cities in the world, 11,532 men and women laughed, cheered and suffered during the greatest folk festival the world has seen.

Chris Brasher finished by wondering:

> Could London stage such a festival? We have a magnificent course ... But do we have the heart and hospitality to welcome the world?

And so it began. In 1981 the first London Marathon was held on 29 March. Over 7,500 runners started (more than 20,000 wanted to run!) and over 6,000 finished. The 1982 event received almost 100,000 would-be marathon runners!

As the London Marathon developed and grew, so too did many other 'big city' marathons around the world; we should remember, however, that the world's oldest running annual marathon event, in Boston, had been in existence since 1897 (founded by the very same American athletes who had competed in the 1896 Olympic Marathon in Greece).

Going past Big Ben at the London Marathon.

The World Marathon Majors

The London and Boston Marathons, together with three other of the biggest city marathons in the world, came together in 2006 to create a series of international marathons; the other three were New York, Chicago and Berlin. The series is known as the World Marathon Majors and is contested by the world's best marathon runners. All five of the races have élite female and male runners, have a mass-participation event at the same time on the same course and have existed for at least 25 years. The races also raise more than $100,000,000 (£67,000,000 sterling) for charity.

Championships

The series also includes any IAAF World Championships and Olympic Games Marathons over a 2-year cycle. Four races at most, and three minimum, count towards the scoring points of 25 (1st), 15 (2nd), 10 (3rd), 5 (4th) and 1 (5th). The World Marathon Majors series is the Grand Prix of marathon running. Each of the five races has history and tradition on their side, and has had the best marathon runners in the world competing in them. The prize money (as well as individual race money) for the series is US$1,000,000 (£670,000 sterling).

These five marathons, plus the Olympic Games Marathons, have had over twenty world records set during them, from Johnny Hayes' (USA) 2h, 55min, 19sec set back in London in 1908, right up to Haile Gebrselassie's (ETH) 2h, 3min, 59sec in Berlin in 2008. Liane Winter (GER) set the inaugural world record for women – when women were finally 'allowed' to compete in marathon running – in Boston in 1975 with 2h, 42min, 24sec, and the record is now held by Great Britain's Paula Radcliffe with her 2h, 15min, 25sec in London in 2003. However this record was set in a 'mixed' race, where Paula was able to take advantage of running with, and being

The Berlin Marathon, going past the Brandenburg Gate.

Finishing the Olympic Games Marathon in the stadium.

The Beijing Olympic Marathon.

paced by, male athletes. She does, however, hold the 'women-only' race record of 2h, 17min, 18sec in Chicago 2002.

It would be very wrong to only consider these 'big five' marathons, particularly if you are looking to enter your first marathon. Certainly the atmosphere at one of the big races can be a big advantage: the crowds of supporters and spectators, the sheer efficiency of the organization, the numbers of other (often more experienced) runners around you can be a big help. However, it can also be a disadvantage. You may get carried away with the atmosphere and start off running too fast; this is one of the cardinal sins of the new marathon runner – start too quickly and you may never recover.

There are many much smaller marathons in Great Britain, and also around the world. Many of my marathon-running friends, and athletes whom I coach, deliberately seek out the smaller, more unusual and even exotic races to enter. They will then use them as a base for a holiday or an exploration of different places. It is also much easier to finish higher up the field in a 'small' marathon. I remember one year when I ran the London Marathon and the Malta Marathon and finished in very similar times. In London I was outside the first thousand, in Malta I was 10th!

CHAPTER 3

HOW TO ENTER

Big or Small?

What will it be then – one of the big, city marathons; or one of the smaller, less well-known marathons? You don't even have to confine yourself to Great Britain; most of the European capital cities and many cities in the United States of America have marathons. Relative ease of road, rail and air travel really does mean that you are spoilt for choice. Entering smaller races is usually straightforward and easy; entering one of the World Marathon Majors can be more difficult.

The London Atmosphere

What do you want from your marathon experience? Is it the thrill of finishing and becoming a marathon runner? My job at the Virgin London Marathon is that of public address and commentator at the 'second' finish line. This is about 200m further on from the finish and is where all the runners come after they have collected their tracksuits and warm clothing. It as an absolute joy for me to talk to runners from Britain and all over the world, from new marathoners to those who have run 20 or 50 or 100 or more, and to listen to them talk about how wonderful London is as a marathon venue. They talk about the encouragement from the crowds, the amazing efficiency at the start lines, the organization of the water, aid and toilet stations around the course, and the sheer friendliness of everyone involved.

Or are you an experienced runner over the shorter distances, and you are looking for a fast time? Are you someone who prefers a flat, fast course? Or are your strengths designed for the hilly, tough courses (like the Snowdonia Marathon that takes in England and Wales' highest peak). The majority of the big city/ Marathon Major events are flat, although Boston does feature 'heartbreak hill' just before the final miles.

When and Where?

You will also have to decide on, and research, likely weather conditions and the course itself. If you're going to run in Arizona in the height of summer, then be prepared for heat. If you choose a northern Scandinavian city towards the onset of winter, then the opposite will apply. Where will you stay before your race? Popular marathons will have lots of athletes there and accommodation may be in short supply. It may be difficult and expensive if your friends and family want to come and support you. Whatever you decide, make it early! You will need a minimum of six months to prepare and train for a marathon, so planning ahead is essential. Use the internet sites; Google the name of the race and almost certainly information will come up. Compare what is offered and what you want, and when you've decided, stick with that decision. As well as researching online, most marathons now accept (and welcome) entries online, although the Virgin London Marathon doesn't. Good race organizers will acknowledge your entry and let you know you've been accepted at least 6 months before the event.

Ballot Entries

Some of the Marathon Majors, including the Virgin London Marathon (and New York), operate a ballot system: you apply for the race and wait to see if your name comes up. For instance, the entries for the 2011 Virgin London Marathon closed in just one day with 125,000 runners wanting to take part. Runners will have been told in the first week of October 2010 whether they have been accepted or not.

The Berlin and Chicago Marathons have an online entry system on a 'first come, first served' basis. It is important to find out when entries open and to enter at the first date indicated.

Boston alone of the big five has an entry time standard dependent on age; if you pass their standard and criteria, then your acceptance is assured.

SAXON SHORE MARATHON ENTRY FORM

Name: ....

Address: ....

....

....

Post Code: ....

Telephone: (day) .... (eve) ....

Emergency contact name and telephone ....

Email: ....

Male/Female: ....

Date of Birth: .... Age (on 10 Dec 2011): ......

UKA/TRA Affiliated Club (or "Unattached"): ....

UKA/TRA Membership No. (if applicable): ....

Saxon Shore Marathon – Saturday 10ᵗʰ December - £40 entry fee ☐

Saxon Shore Marathon – Sunday 11ᵗʰ December - £40 entry fee ☐

Hardcore Option – Both Marathons - £70 entry fee ☐

Technical T-Shirt – Please circle required size (unisex sizes) – S   M   L   XL

Signature: .... Date: ....

Cheques made payable to: **Traviss Willcox**

Send your entries to: Saxon Shore Marathon, 8 The Glen, Shepherdswell, Dover, Kent, CT15 7PF

Competitors must be at least 18 years of age on the day of the event. A signed form will be considered as a declaration that you will run entirely at your own risk and that you have no medical disabilities that would endanger you or others taking part. Entry fees are non refundable. In the event of cancellation, all proceeds will go to charity.
A confirmed entry list will be posted on the www.saxon-shore.com site, if your cheque clears then you are in!

A typical marathon entry form.

Charity Entries

It is obvious that getting accepted into the big races is not easy. One way is to run for a charity. Many charities have taken on board that sponsored marathon running is a fantastic way of generating revenue. London and other major events will hold a number of reserved, guaranteed-entry places and sell them to the charities. The charity will then give, or sell, these entries to runners, who in turn guarantee that they will raise a certain amount of money for the charity. It is an arrangement that benefits everyone. Googling the marathon sites on the internet will give many different charities that you can apply to directly. There are various different criteria for different charities.

Clearly it is essential that, once you have accepted a place through a charity, you must commit to proper preparation and training. Not finishing is not an option when you can, quite literally, have hundreds or thousands of pounds riding on your success at completing the 26.2 miles. However, injury is another matter. If you are injured or ill, under no circumstances should you run! If it becomes obvious that you will not be fit and healthy on the race day, withdraw as early as possible so that the race organizers or charities can allocate your place to someone on the waiting lists.

Entering a Half-Marathon

Similarly, when entering a half-marathon, the 'big' races will fill up first. Do your research, find out – as with the full-marathon entries – which system is going to work best for you, and enter as soon as possible.

Running for a charity can help you get an entry to the popular marathons.

CHAPTER 4

SHOES, CLOTHING AND EQUIPMENT

Running Shoes

The single most important piece of equipment that you will need is a pair of running shoes. Choosing a pair is far more difficult than it might appear, as there are well over 250 different types and models of running shoe available. The most important factor is that I, you, we, all of us are individuals with differences in weight, height, running style, body make-up and a myriad of other factors, which make us just that – individual athletes with individual needs and requirements.

It is not necessary to buy an expensive pair of running shoes to start with; what is important is that you go to a reputable specialist running shop and take advice from people who know about running and will help you choose what is best for you, not what is best for the shop. However, it is worthwhile knowing something about running shoes and how these features will affect your running.

Today's running shoes' uppers are almost always made of nylon, which is lighter than leather, dries more quickly and retains shape better than leather. How you lace up running shoes is important because it can relieve pressure on the feet. Always take advice from the experts in the running shop.

The Outer Sole

This is that part that comes into contact with the ground on every footfall. The outer sole should be long-lasting and have good grip. The outer sole should also give good cushioning and shock absorption – particularly for heavier runners. However, if the sole is very soft, giving good cushioning, then it is likely to wear down fairly quickly.

Depending on the gait and foot-strike of the runner, many athletes will find that the outside of the heel wears down very quickly, this occurs naturally when the runner is a heel-striker. Although some runners will get their shoes repaired on this heel-strike, it is probably best to allow the heel to wear naturally, as it is only accommodating the individual runner's natural running action. Repairing the shoe will only mean re-continued wear on the heel.

The Midsole

The midsole lies between the road contact (outer sole) and the body of the shoe itself; it lessens and absorbs the pounding and landing of the foot as it makes contact with the ground, it stabilizes the foot, and flexes across from side to side (i.e. not from heel to toes). Many running shoes have tiny gas bubbles injected into the midsole material making the shoe light and a good shock absorber. However, with constant wear, the bubbles are flattened and pushed out, making the midsole harder and less shock absorbent.

The two functions of stabilizing the foot, while still allowing flexion, work against each other, and the experienced runner will know which is the more important for them. The new runner will also quickly come to realize where their priorities are.

Slip- or Board-Lasting Running Shoes

These terms apply to how the upper part of the shoe is attached to the midsole. The upper part of the shoe is stitched and then glued on to the midsole; if it is glued directly, it is known as slip-lasting, if a board is fitted between the upper and midsole it is known as board-lasting. Shoes that are board-lasted are best for runners who need stability, while slip-lasted shoes apply to runners who are okay with movement.

The Heel Counter

Around the heel on the upper shoe there is strong plastic (usually) that helps to maintain stability when running. Runners who require a shoe that will limit pronation and mobility should choose a shoe with a firm heel counter

Straight- or Curved-Lasting

Straight-lasted shoes are symmetrical around a plumb-line from middle of the heel to the middle of the toe; a curved-lasted shoe bends inwards to the middle of the forefoot. Straight-lasted shoes are good for runners who require movement control; curved-lasted shoes are good for runners who need foot movement and shock absorption.

Buying Your Shoes

Buy running shoes in the afternoon, as your feet swell approximately half a size during the day. Make sure there is a little space between your longest toe and the front of the shoe (approximately a centimetre). Your toes should have enough room to 'wiggle'. Your new shoes have to feel 'good' on you when you buy them; if they're uncomfortable in the shop, they won't feel any better when you're at home.

Heel counter

Mid sole →

Outer sole

← Toe box

Features of a running shoe.

Socks, Pants and Bras

The wrong socks can cause blisters! As with most running clothes, the new technology has ensured that (almost) blister-resistant socks are available; they are made with two layers of fabric, thus ensuring that the friction rub is against each other rather than against the skin. Two layers of fabric also get rid of sweat more easily. Also, some sock manufacturers now make differently shaped socks for the left and right feet. It may seem like a tiny bit of attention to detail, but all these advantages are worth having over 26 miles. Some athletes choose not to wear socks and this is a personal choice. However, if you normally do wear socks, under no circumstances choose to experiment by not wearing them on a long race or training run. Many (even most) triathletes run with no socks, but this is because of the nature of the sport, where time taken in putting them on during transition will be time wasted. However, triathletes in Ironman competitions, where the running distance is a marathon, often will take that extra transition time and wear socks

Underpants should be light and close-fitting without being too tight, many running shorts for both men and women now have built-in pants that are light and made especially for running.

If socks and pants need attention to detail, it is even more crucial with specialist sports bras. The correct size (once again close-fitting but not over-tight) with excellent support is paramount. Rigid bras are necessary, particularly for women with large breasts. Bra straps should be fairly wide to avoid cutting into the skin and non-elastic and non-slip, while the bra cups should also be non-elastic with no raised seams or metal or plastic fasteners next to the skin. The breasts should be held close to the body without being over-tight. The bottom of the bra (underneath the bra cups) should have a wide cloth band to avoid the bra slipping up while running. Don't be tempted to keep a bra for too long a period of time. With a lot of running use, they will wear fairly quickly and need replacing at least every six months or so.

Clothing

In general it is best to choose light running vests or T-shirts and shorts. The body while running produces an enormous amount of heat and heavy clothing will only make it more difficult to get rid of that heat, let alone the sweat that is produced. Of course, in very cold conditions it is essential to dress appropriately for running with a tracksuit or sweatshirt and leggings (tights). It is a misconception that running in heavy clothing will make you lose a lot of weight; all that is lost is extra sweat and the water weight lost will go back on as soon as you drink after training. Also, it is preferable to wear several layers of light clothing on top of each other in cold weather, rather than one very heavy item – the heat and moisture will disperse more quickly and easily.

Wearing nice, light, well-fitting, attractive clothing will make you feel better in training and during racing. Shorts and tops that fit poorly will rub, irritate and cut your skin. Ensure that you have everything going for you by having the correct clothing.

Shorts

Be comfortable! Buy the correct size and make sure they don't have raised seams or edges that will cut into your inside thighs and ensure that you're not able to train for several days. Shorts that have underpants sewn in are available and are a matter of personal choice. Don't buy a pair of shorts where the legs are too long, they will make you feel uncomfortable and slow you down.

Vest and T-Shirts

The material should be light, preferably not heavy cotton. Nylon or similar material should allow sweat and heat to be easily dispersed. (This dispersal of sweat, moisture and heat is known as 'wicking'.) Be aware that a too tight-fitting vest is likely to cause irritation on the nipples (more on men than women as women will be wearing a bra) and may even cause bleeding. Conversely, a vest that is too loose may also create problems.

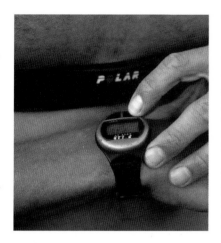

Heart rate monitor strapped to the chest.

BUYING TIPS

- Take advice from experienced runners and specialist running shops.
- Don't always buy top-of-the-range.
- Whatever it is … make sure it fits.
- Don't stint on shoes and clothing, you'll appreciate the comfort.

The Extras

For cold-weather training, a pair of running tights is preferable to tracksuit bottoms. An added bonus is that they may keep injury away, as they support the leg muscles – particularly important when cold. As with other clothing, breathable fabric is preferable.

If you do need to wear warm tops, keep them light in weight. Be aware that rain will be absorbed if the wrong material is chosen and that will make running unpleasant. A light jacket with perhaps a rain-jacket over the top is best for wet-weather running.

Gloves and a hat are great assets during the winter, possibly even more important than a warm top. One-third of body heat is lost through the top of the head and the warmth of your hands can dictate how pleasant or unpleasant a run will be. Light gloves are usually sufficient. A hat with a sun visor (a baseball-type hat) can be useful in hot, sunny weather, as will sunglasses. If you do wear sunglasses, ensure they are tight, cut out any glare and will not slip up and down the face, especially when sweating.

Other things to consider buying are a heart rate monitor (HRM) (see Chapter 5) and a training diary. An HRM can give you instant feedback on your training and your efforts, but be warned that it is not an instant panacea and that heart rates can be affected by several things – including illness – as well as training exertions. HRMs are now excellent value and entry-level monitors can be as little as £30. Most runners keep training diaries, but how many use them properly? For many, it is merely a book to record the training done. For the intelligent diary-keeper, it's a record of what sessions preceded the best race, which sessions were immediately before a poor race, i.e. an indication of what works best in training.

A water-bottle can be a help and a hindrance. It is necessary to keep hydrated during running but carrying a bottle with you can slightly alter your running technique and can more easily lead to injury. Better to have planned water stops during

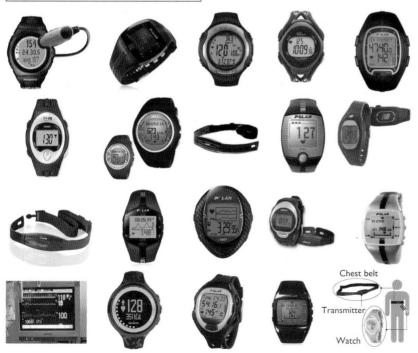

Different heart rate monitors.

The Timex Global Trainer.

training. During races, water should be available at drinking stations. It may sound silly, but it is well worth practising drinking on the run during a training session. It is a complex skill to begin with!

One relatively new piece of equipment that has impressed me is the Timex Global Trainer. It is an 'all-in-one' watch, HRM, distance and time calculator, and even a global positioning system (GPS). It really is invaluable on those long running sessions in strange or new locations. Training to heart-rate zones is good, but also training at 'race pace' will provide good benefits in terms of familiarizing the runner to the pace of their target marathon time (see Chapter 7). Increasingly, accomplished marathon runners are training different sessions to training zones calculated either from heart-rate zone and other sessions based on speed or pace zones. The data monitored by the speed/distance mode are also invaluable for communicating to yourself and your coach just how much mileage you are actually achieving.

Appropriate clothing for difficult conditions.

PART II
TRAINING AND TECHNIQUES

CHAPTER 5

EXERCISE PHYSIOLOGY

An understanding of the basics in the area of exercise physiology is invaluable to runners and to coaches. The principles of exercise physiology provide the base for marathon and half-marathon running training programmes and enable the runner and coach to work out appropriate training for each individual.

It is important to clarify the definitions and terms used in exercise physiology.

TERMS AND DEFINITIONS

- **Aerobic**: 'with oxygen', i.e. the presence of oxygen is essential
- **Anaerobic**: 'without oxygen', i.e. anaerobic processes do not require the presence of oxygen but an anaerobic process can take place even if there is plenty of oxygen around
- **Oxygen debt**: this is the increased oxygen taken in after the athlete has stopped exercising

---

Energy Systems

For a muscle to be able to contract, there must be a source of energy available. The body's energy carrier is a molecule called ATP (adenosine triphosphate) and a constant supply of ATP is required by the body. There are five systems in our bodies by which ATP can be generated: four are anaerobic, i.e. don't require oxygen and the other is aerobic, i.e. sufficient oxygen must be present. For marathon and half-marathon runners, it is predominantly the aerobic system that is relevant. However, at top level, there is an increasing need for the anaerobic systems to be trained as well.

We should not think that energy-producing reactions work independently of each other – which reaction predominates will depend on the intensity and duration of the exercise. The anaerobic systems can produce ATP very quickly but at a cost (the athlete is soon fatigued); the aerobic

---

ENERGY SYSTEMS

Anaerobic Energy Systems

1. ATP stores in the muscles.
2. Creatine phosphate stores in the muscles.
3. ADP + ADP, ATP + AMP.
4. Glycogen ATP + lactic acid.

Aerobic Energy System

5. Carbohydrates, fats + O_2 > ATP + water + carbon dioxide

---

reaction takes longer to generate ATP but can produce very large amounts for long periods of time.

The Aerobic System

The two main fuel sources for the aerobic system are carbohydrates and fats. Carbohydrates are stored in the body as glycogen in the liver and in the muscles; also, glucose circulates in the bloodstream. Fats are stored as triglycerides in various sites in the body, including the muscles. Triglycerides consist of a glycerol molecule to which three fatty acid molecules are attached. When fats are needed as a fuel, the triglyceride molecules split up into glycerol and FFA (free fatty acids).

The glycogen stored in the liver is broken down into glucose by a process called glycogenolysis; the glucose enters the bloodstream and is taken to the working muscles. Here, the glucose from the blood and from the muscle's own supplies of glycogen (which also undergo glycogenolysis) is changed to glucose-6-phosphate and enters the process of glycolysis.

The end-product of glycolysis is pyruvic acid. This substance then enters the

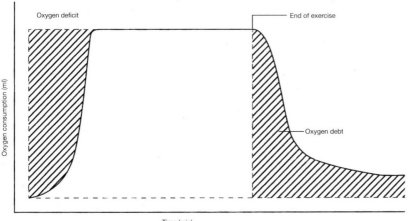

Oxygen deficit

End of exercise

Oxygen consumption (ml)

Oxygen debt

Time (min)

Oxygen debt.

mitochondria (the 'engine rooms' of the muscle) and is eventually converted to water and carbon dioxide, and in the process leads to the formation of ATP.

While some ATP is produced by glycolysis, the reactions in the mitochondria (which are known as the Krebs cycle or the citric acid cycle (TCA) cycle) create much greater quantities of ATP. But, glycolysis doesn't need oxygen to take place – the reactions in the mitochondria do require the presence of oxygen, otherwise they soon stop. As the production of ATP from FFA occurs in the mitochondria (via the same processes as pyruvic acid), oxygen must be available for FFA to be used as a fuel.

The use of fats, in addition to carbohydrates, as a fuel source has advantages over just using carbohydrates. Fats yield more energy, weight for weight, than carbohydrates (fats: 39kJ/g, glucose 16.7kJ/g). The body is also able to store far greater quantities of fat than glycogen. It is estimated that, if each fuel was used by itself, then glycogen stores would last about 90min while fats could keep us going for more than 50h! This is very relevant to marathon runners, where the fastest in the world will run for just over two hours; if fat were not available (and having been used in training previously), then the runner would be out of energy well before the finish. This used to be called 'the bonk' or 'hitting the wall'.

There is a drawback in using fats: to release the same amount of energy, fats need more oxygen than carbohydrates. So if a runner is training at a particular speed, more oxygen would be needed than if only using carbohydrate. By using fats, the runner will need to use less glycogen to run at the same speed and the role of the oxygen transport system becomes important.

The Oxygen (O_2) Transport System

The O_2 transport system is the lungs, heart, blood vessels and blood (the cardio-respiratory system). The purpose of the cardio-respiratory system is to transport oxygen to the parts of the body that need

it and to remove the resultant carbon dioxide produced.

The lungs provide the mechanism by which the oxygen in the air we breathe is transferred into the blood. The air enters the trachea (windpipe) through the nose and mouth; the trachea divides into two bronchi: one enters the left lung, while the other goes into the right lung. In the lungs, the bronchi carry on dividing until the alveoli (air sacs) are reached. The exchange of gases (O_2 and CO_2) between the lungs and the blood vessels takes place in the alveoli.

Generally with breathing, it is more efficient to take deeper but less frequent breaths, rather than breathing shallowly but quickly.

While the lungs are obviously important for taking in air, their capacity is not greatly increased by training (10 per cent at the most). The amount of oxygen available for exchange in the alveoli is only very slightly increased, if at all. But the system for transporting the oxygen – the cardiovascular system – does show great improvements with training.

The cardiac output (the amount of blood pumped by the heart) is governed by heart rate and stroke volume – this is the volume of blood pumped by each beat of the heart.

Cardiac Output = Heart Rate × Stroke Volume.

Training does not raise the maximum heart rate (it can actually fall) of a runner, but the stroke volume will be greatly increased. So the same cardiac output can be achieved at a lower heart rate, as due

to the runner's increased stroke volume, more blood is pumped by each beat of the heart.

Additionally, aerobic training causes more blood vessels to form in the muscles and the amount of blood in the body rises. The greater volume of blood means there is more haemoglobin – the molecule that carries oxygen around the body.

But while training leads to increases in the amount of oxygen transported by the cardio-respiratory system, there is still a limit to how much oxygen can be carried to, and used by, the muscles.

VO_2max

An athlete running will use more oxygen than at rest, i.e. their oxygen uptake rises. At any particular work intensity for that individual, the oxygen uptake will reach a plateau – the maximal oxygen uptake or VO_2max per minute. If the runner exercises at a greater intensity (runs faster), his/her oxygen uptake will not increase because the body is now taking in and using all the oxygen it can.

Maximal oxygen uptake is most accurately assessed in a physiology laboratory using a gas analyser that measures the levels of oxygen in the air breathed in and out by the athlete. Other, less accurate, methods of measurement are available and provide information that can be used by runners and coaches, with a degree of caution.

If the figure produced by testing is divided by the individual's body weight, the VO_2max value can be expressed in terms

---

HOW VO_2MAX IS CALCULATED

VO_2max = Maximum Cardiac Output × a – VO_2 difference,

where:

Maximum Cardiac Output = Maximum Heart Rate × Maximum Stroke Volume.

a – VO_2 difference = oxygen content of arterial blood – oxygen content of venous blood.

VO_2max is also known as maximal aerobic power. Maximal aerobic capacity is different – it is equivalent to the anaerobic threshold.

of millilitres of oxygen used per minute per kilogram of bodyweight (ml/min/kg). This allows comparisons to be made between athletes.

VO_2max values will vary depending on the runner's age, sex and fitness level.

While VO_2max is often used to assess aerobic fitness, it must be remembered that athletes with a similar performance level can have very different VO_2max scores, while athletes with similar VO_2max values can have very different performance levels.

Training can lead to increases in a runner's VO_2max (15 to 20 per cent) but the improvements seem to be limited by genetic factors. But although a runner, after a regular training programme, may only show a small rise in their VO_2max result, their endurance capacity may have vastly improved. The runner is now able to exercise at a greater percentage of their VO_2max without becoming fatigued. This level of intensity has been called the anaerobic threshold.

Exercise Thresholds

Aerobic Threshold

There are two important exercise thresholds relevant to runners. The lower (easier) of the two is the aerobic threshold. Above this threshold, the adaptations in the body, resulting from training, take place, e.g. increased numbers of mitochondria, better blood supply to the muscles. Below the aerobic threshold, very few significant changes occur in the body. So the training load must be at an intensity greater than the runner's aerobic threshold before training effects will appear.

Anaerobic Threshold

At the beginning of this section, the energy systems that produce ATP were outlined. As the runner increases their running speed, more and more of the ATP needed will be produced by anaerobic metabolism. It is not correct to think that at a certain running speed, the runner switches from using solely aerobic mechanisms to only using anaerobic energy supply.

The intensity at which anaerobic metabolism starts to make a significant contribution to ATP production has been called the anaerobic threshold (AT). (The AT will be lower than VO_2max in all athletes.)

There has been, and still is, a lot of discussion in exercise physiology about the concept of the anaerobic threshold. But clearly there is a certain exercise intensity above which a runner will fatigue quickly and have to slow down. At work intensities greater than the AT, lactic acid starts to accumulate and breathing becomes more strained. The intensity at which the breathing rate dramatically changes is called the ventilatory threshold (VT or T vent). Other names for the anaerobic threshold that you might come across are: lactate threshold (T lac) and OBLA (onset of blood lactate accumulation) – but OBLA is not always the same as the anaerobic threshold. OBLA is taken to be a specific concentration of lactate (4mm/ltr) for everyone and does not change with training, although the work intensity at which OBLA occurs can change.

For a runner, the ideal is to race just below his/her anaerobic threshold with short periods when the threshold is crossed, i.e. running up a hill.

Heart Rate and Heart Rate Monitors

The heart rate response to intense exercise is nearly immediate. The higher the intensity of the exercise, the higher the heart rate. Even in non-sprint events, heart rates for trained athletes of 180bpm are common within 30sec of the start of a 1- or 2-mile run. After this quick increase in heart rate, further increases are more gradual, usually with several plateaus being reached during the run. This intense response is common. For marathon and half-marathon races, extreme caution should be taken not to allow the heart rate to get too high too quickly.

Both the aerobic and anaerobic thresholds can be expressed as percentages of a runner's VO_2max value, i.e. as an oxygen uptake figure such as 3ltr/min, or as work intensity, e.g. 300 watts. Both these types of guidelines have their practical drawbacks, and in recent years, runners have started to use heart rate and heart rate monitors as an indication of training thresholds. This is because heart rate linearly increases with the rise in intensity of exercise (this relationship breaks down as the runner approaches his/her maximal oxygen uptake).

The use of heart rates to gauge training and racing intensities is appealing, but heart rates should not be used as the sole indicator of training/racing intensity. The following points should be remembered by both the coach and the runner:

1   **Accuracy**: for the runner to know whether they are running near their anaerobic threshold, the heart rate must be measured during the run, not when the runner has stopped. It is impossible for the runner to accurately and safely measure their own heart rate when running hard on public roads. Therefore, a heart rate monitor has to be used and one that is accurate and reliable, i.e. not a fingertip or ear-lobe model.

    Personal factors: each of us is a unique individual – one of the drawbacks of exercise physiology is that generalized results are calculated and this can cause problems. An example is the estimation of a person's maximum heart rate by subtracting their age from 220. Taking a maximal exercise test will give more accurate results.

2   **The loading factor** in the Karvonen formula will be different for many runners from those given (0.7 and 0.85). For the less fit runner, the anaerobic threshold may be reached at 50 per cent of their maximum heart rate (a loading factor of 0.5). The loading factor has to be estimated for each runner.

    Overtraining can increase your resting heart rate, as can a rise in your perceived stress levels. The

---

THE KARVONEN FORMULA

This can be used to calculate the heart rates (HR) that correspond to a runner's aerobic and anaerobic thresholds:

Heart Rate = Loading Factor × (Maximum HR − Resting HR) + Resting HR

where:

Loading Factor = percentage of maximum heart rate that coincides with the threshold to be determined.

(Normal loading factors are 0.7 for the aerobic threshold, i.e. 70 per cent of maximum heart rate and 0.85 for the anaerobic threshold, i.e. 85 per cent of the maximum heart rate. However, it must be emphasized that some individual runners will vary greatly on these percentage levels.)

If we take a runner with a resting heart rate of 55 beats per minute (bpm) and a maximum heart rate of 185 beats per minute, then the Karvonen formula gives us the following answers:

Aerobic threshold = 0.7 × (185 − 55) + 55
= 0.7 × 130 + 55
= 91 + 55
= 146bpm.

Anaerobic threshold = 0.85 × (185 − 55) + 55
= 0.85 × 130 + 55
= 110.5 + 55
= 165.5 bpm (round down to 165 bpm).

(Maximum heart rate can be estimated by subtracting the runner's age from 220; again, this is a generalization and may well often be inaccurate.)

---

taking of certain medications can also influence heart rates.

3 Environmental factors: these include temperature, humidity and altitude. In a hot and humid climate, until the runner is acclimatized, heart rates will be higher than normal at a given work intensity. This is because more of the blood is diverted to the skin surface to promote cooling; therefore, the heart has to work harder to provide the working muscles with the required volume of blood.

4 Fluid intake/cooling: all runners should ensure that they have an adequate intake of liquids before, during and after exercise. During hot weather, using water to cool the body by splashing it on can also help. By being hydrated in training and racing, the runner will be able to exercise at a higher pulse rate before fatiguing.

5 Reassessment: it is important to regularly assess a runner's progress, but even more so when heart rates are used to decide on training/racing intensity. As the runner improves, the heart rates that correspond to the aerobic and anaerobic thresholds will change. If runners don't regularly test themselves, they may train at the wrong intensity. A heart rate should only be used as a guideline and the runner should learn to recognize when they are training and racing at the appropriate intensity.

Finding Maximum Heart Rate (MHR)

There are a number of different tests and methods for testing MHR; two are described here.

The 12-Minute Test

Also known as the VO$_2$max test, this is a test that can be repeated as needed to determine improvement in your conditioning. Cooper, in his original book *Aerobics*, developed the procedures for the 12-minute run test. After warming up, run at an even pace for at least 10min and then at an all-out pace for the last 2min. Measure the total distance covered during the 12min. As fitness improves, you should be able to cover a longer distance in the same amount of time.

Graduated Test

Take your best 1-mile time. Start at a pace one minute per mile slower than your fastest predicted 1-mile time. Then, gradually increase the pace such that by the fourth lap you are at your top 1-mile speed, and then give it all you've got for that last 200m.

Illness/Overtraining

Heart rate monitors can be used to alert athletes that they are training at intensities, frequencies or durations that are too demanding. Overtraining is common with athletes who believe more is better and don't take a systematic approach to training. One of the best indications of overtraining is your morning resting HR. If this is 10bpm higher than normal, there may be a concern. A high resting HR could indicate that you may be overtraining, suffering from fatigue, slightly injured or fighting off a virus or a stress-related problem. There is a simple solution: rest.

A number of problems can arise during training or racing; these can sometimes be more easily diagnosed by using your HR monitor. A checklist is included in the box overleaf.

Racing with a Heart Rate Monitor

Some of the most valuable HR information comes from racing. The information after the race can reveal a tremendous amount of information as to fitness levels, signs of overtraining and whether race pacing has been good.

If we know our anaerobic threshold (in my case it correlates to an 83–86 per cent effort when unfit and a 90–92 per cent effort when fit), we can use a monitor to pace ourselves. In a short race (less than 1 hour, e.g. 10km running race), we can maintain a heart rate 3–5 beats above our anaerobic threshold. For a longer race (i.e. marathon or half-marathon) we will be 3–5 beats below anaerobic threshold. A good race graph should be roughly even throughout. If the graph tails off in the later stages of the race, we have started too fast or we were insufficiently rested for the race. If the graph starts to go up in the later stages, it may indicate dehydration or hyperthermia (overheating) – watch your liquid!

Muscle-Fibre Types

There are three types of muscles fibres: slow twitch and two types of fast twitch (recent research suggests there may be more). The slow twitch takes longer to contract than the fast twitch. The differences between the fibres are:

- **Slow twitch**: also called slow oxidative, red or Type 1 fibres. These have a plentiful supply of blood carried by a dense network of capillaries (the tiny blood vessels in the muscle), hence the name 'red', and therefore can receive great quantities of oxygen and fuel, and any waste products can also be quickly flushed away. Additionally, these fibres have great numbers of mitochondria and high concentrations of the enzymes required in aerobic metabolism. These factors make slow-twitch fibres ideal for aerobic energy production as they can repeatedly contract, without fatiguing, for many hours.
- **Fast twitch:** also called white or Type 2 fibres. The two types are Type 2A (fast oxidative glycolytic) and Type 2B (fast glycolytic). While both types have fewer capillaries in comparison with slow-twitch fibres, Type 2A fibres can work aerobically or anaerobically; Type 2B fibres mainly work anaerobically. Fast-twitch fibres are adapted to producing ATP quickly but they fatigue far more quickly than slow-twitch fibres.

Your muscles don't consist of exclusively one type but of a mixture of all three. The percentage of each fibre type in the muscle will differ from person to person. People with a higher percentage of slow-twitch fibres in their muscles will be more suited to endurance events like marathons and half-marathons.

Muscle-fibre type should not be thought of as a way to exclude people from certain sports because their muscle-fibre mix is 'wrong'. Enjoyment and satisfaction are the important factors.

When a muscle is working, the slow-twitch fibres will be used first, at low loads; then the Type 2A fibres are brought in as the work gets harder. Finally, with a further increase in intensity, the Type 2B fibres start being employed.

Lactic Acid

As with oxygen debt, there are a number of misconceptions about lactic acid (also called lactate):

- Lactic acid is not a 'poison'. Even at rest, there is a small quantity of the substance circulating in the bloodstream – normally about 1 millimole of lactate per litre of blood (1mmol/ltr). Muscles (slow-twitch type) and other organs in the body (e.g. the heart) are also capable of converting lactic acid into pyruvic acid, which can then enter the Krebs cycle.
- Lactic acid is not only produced when there is a lack of oxygen in the muscles. Lactate production also occurs when fast-twitch muscles are used and when more pyruvate is produced than can enter the Krebs cycle.
- Increased production does not automatically mean that there will be a higher concentration of lactate, because the concentration depends not only on rate of production, but also on the rate of removal and conversion.
- Lactic acid is not the cause of the pain in the muscles the day after exercising. The acid is cleared away and converted relatively quickly, especially if the runner properly warms down. The reason for the painful sensations (called delayed onset muscle soreness or DOMS) is not definitely known, but leakage of fluids and other substances are believed to be the main causes.

There have been suggestions that optimal endurance training effects take place at a lactate concentration of 4mmol/ltr but there is too much variability between athletes for a single value to be valid for everyone. Runners should only use lactate measures as one indicator of training intensity, not as the sole measure.

Fatigue

The main reason for a runner having to slow down near the end of a race is not due to the build-up of lactic acid; it is because the runner's glycogen stores have been seriously depleted and they are having to rely more on fats as the fuel source. Therefore, pacing is a crucial factor in successful distance racing (there are other causes of fatigue in distance running but glycogen depletion is the central reason).

While a runner might expect to always feel fatigued during everyday training, the athlete or coach should avoid this situation, especially with novice runners. Many long-distance runners overtrain and would enjoy themselves more and achieve better race results if they heeded the other part of training.

Recovery

Training sessions of a high intensity lead to glycogen depletion and it can take up to 48h for the glycogen levels to return to normal. This is one of the reasons for having a recovery session the day after a hard training run.

Because of these adaptations, the runner is able to use fats at an earlier stage when exercising; the muscles are able to use more oxygen; more ATP is produced aerobically; and the point at which lactic acid starts to accumulate is delayed.

The runner will probably have a higher maximum oxygen uptake value and will have raised their anaerobic threshold and so be able to perform at a greater percentage of their VO_2max for a longer period of time.

Implications for Training

From the previous sections, we can now see that the aim of training is to cause changes in the cardiovascular system and improvements in aerobic muscle endurance (local muscular endurance). Any form of aerobic training will lead to the stated adaptations in the cardiovascular system (factors 2, 3 and 4). But the physiological changes in aerobic muscle endurance (factors 5, 6, 7 and 8) are confined to the muscles used in that training session.

By mixing different types of training sessions, runners will improve their cardiovascular system and their local muscular endurance. (See Chapter 7 for further explanation.)

Implications for Racing

With some knowledge of exercise physiology, we can make suggestions to our runners about racing.

The main watchword is pacing. The athlete must run at a speed appropriate to their level of fitness on that day and the distance of the race (marathon, half-marathon or shorter). If the runner works at too high an intensity, they will go over their anaerobic threshold; fatigue results and the runner has to slow down. Remember that speed may not be the only direct measure of intensity: weather, terrain and local conditions can all affect speed.

Other Points

At the start, the runner must be careful not to sprint away. While some lactic acid will be produced at these times in a race, by setting a sensible pace the runner will avoid accumulating large amounts and will also spare their glycogen stores. Similarly, on hills and when trying to break away from a competitor, the runner is likely to be working at an intensity above their anaerobic threshold. In these situations, the runner will have to gauge the amount of time they can afford at that increased intensity – the distance left to race, the

ADAPTATIONS TO TRAINING

The following ten adaptations occur due to endurance training:

1 Greatly improved neuromuscular functions – more fibres contract together and with greater efficiency.
2 Increased heart stroke volume – therefore a higher cardiac output for the same heart rate as prior to training.
3 Increase in number of red blood cells (so more haemoglobin).
4 Increase in the volume of blood in the body.
5 Greater number of capillaries in the muscles.
6 Increased amount of myoglobin in the muscle fibres. Myoglobin is the molecule that transports and stores oxygen in muscle cells.
7 The number of mitochondria in the muscle fibres increases.
8 The fast-twitch muscle fibres' capacity to produce ATP aerobically greatly improves; principally that of the Type 2A fibres.
9 The runner starts to sweat sooner when exercising.
10 The runner's sweat is more dilute – about a 50 per cent reduction in the concentration of sodium, potassium, magnesium and chloride in the sweat.

NB Points 3 and 4 may lead to the distance runner being diagnosed as anaemic, i.e. having a lower than normal concentration of haemoglobin. Although the total amount of haemoglobin is greater than before training, the increase does not match the rise in blood volume and consequently the concentration of haemoglobin is reduced.

EXCELLENCE IN PERFORMANCE

1 A high, but not phenomenal VO_2max.
2 The ability to utilize a high percentage of VO_2max for sustained periods.
3 The ability to sustain high power outputs and resist muscle fatigue during prolonged exercise.
4 A high-power output at the lactate threshold.
5 An efficient technique.
6 The ability to utilize fat as a fuel during sustained exercise at high work rates.

Time on the feet is what counts.

severity of the rest of the course and the state of the runner should influence the decision.

Fatigue resistance is simply the ability of the runner to resist fatigue during a long race (or, how much can I hurt?). This is the major adaptation to distance-running training.

Excellent technique or economy of movement (or, how well do you run?). The best endurance runners are usually the most efficient, with the suggestions that high weekly running mileage increases running efficiency; including a decrease in stride length and increase in stride frequency

Final note: sports science is not an exact science (and never will be). However, runners who don't acknowledge the benefits of exercise physiology may not make the best use out of the coaching and running expertise. Exercise physiology is not something that is divorced from everyday training and racing; it is used for the good of the runner.

CHAPTER 6

BASIC TRAINING

If you are a 'new' runner, the first stages of training are not necessarily to become fit, but rather to establish the habit of regular exercise. This initial stage may be between six and twelve weeks. It is important to have short- and long-term goals in mind – if not, then why start training? The long-term goal is very likely to be running a half- or full marathon (or why are you reading this book?); the short-term goal(s) will be to cover a certain distance or run for a certain period of time each day or week.

Many, many would-be full and half-marathon runners never fulfil either goal because they set out in training too hard! They attempt to do too much, too soon. Your legs, tendons and joints will not be accustomed to the jarring and pounding of running. Rule one, make haste slowly! If you try to start too quickly, you will get injured.

Getting Started

Once you are confirmed medically healthy to begin an exercise and running pro-gramme, it is important to set out exactly when and what you are aiming for. There are a lot of beginner marathon-training programmes in many would-be maratho-ner books, and in a lot of ways the training programmes for new runners set out will be very similar. Many of them propose being able to run (finish) a marathon after 6 months of training, and a half-marathon in even less time than that. I feel that this is a very ambitious schedule. Certainly, it may be possible to finish a marathon on that 24 weeks'/6 months' training and a half-marathon on 16 weeks' training; however, it is necessary to ask three questions:

1   Will I enjoy the experience?
2   How will I feel at the end of the race?
3   Will I want to run another marathon?

I believe that it is more realistic to set out a 'new marathoner' schedule over at least 36 weeks (perhaps even longer) and a new half-marathoner schedule of 30 weeks, giving at least 50 per cent more time to prepare. Within that time, there should be racing targets set to check how progress is going, to include a 6-mile/10,000m race and – for the full marathon – a half-marathon. The extra

---

FIT TO TRAIN

It is essential that you are healthy; the American College of Sports Medicine and the US National Heart, Lung and Blood Institute advise that there are eight criteria to be healthy (and safe) enough to start exercising or training.

1   Over 60 years old and not accustomed to vigorous exercise.
2   A family history of premature coronary artery disease.
3   Frequent pains or pressure in the left or mid-chest area; left neck, shoulder or arm during or immediately after exercise.
4   Feeling faint or severe dizziness, extreme breathlessness after mild exercise.
5   High blood pressure or not knowing if your blood pressure is normal.
6   A history of heart trouble, heart murmur, a previous heart attack.
7   Arthritis, bone or joint problems.
8   Another medical condition such as insulin-dependent diabetes.

Whatever the conditions, when you have started training it's important to keep it going.

Basic training can be done anywhere.

Time on Your Feet

Some experienced running coaches and experienced runners also talk about the importance of running for the period of time that you anticipate taking for the half- or full marathon. Importantly, it is not necessary to run for whatever period of time you are aiming for at that race speed, but rather to know what the feeling of being on your feet for three or four or five hours is like. As an example, an inexperienced marathon runner who is aiming for a finishing time of 4h would be looking at an average speed of 6½mph, a pace/speed of 9min for each mile. For that 4h training run, the pace would be slower, perhaps 11min per mile, so that 22 miles would be covered in that long preparation training run.

12 weeks will allow a lot of preparation time that can include walking and give the body adequate time for adjustment to a weekly schedule that is likely, eventually, to include at least 7h of running each week.

It is unrealistic to expect to be able to finish a half- or full marathon in a reasonable state unless you have covered at least twice the running time (preferably nearer three times) over a period of seven days.

Preparation is Everything

A recent survey of 'new' and 'charity' runners (Raven 2010) who achieved their target marathon time, shows that 89 per cent of those achieving their target time for the marathon had run at least 500 miles in the previous six months. This averages out to 20 miles per week, and assuming that they gradually built up the mileage; it is likely that they were running between 30 and 40 miles each week in the final few weeks before their target race. Even more significantly, of new marathoners who had run double that distance – 1,000 miles in the previous six months, an average of 40

Even a dried up river bed gives training opportunities!

PREPARATION – SOME STATISTICS

- Less than 500 miles in 6 months before marathon – success rate 21 per cent.
- More than 500 miles in 6 months before marathon – success rate 89 per cent.
- More than 1000 miles in 6 months before marathon– success rate 98 per cent.

Run anywhere, it doesn't have to be pretty.

miles per week and a likely 60 miles each week in the final preparations – only 2 per cent did not achieve their target time. Assuming a certain illness factor and things that didn't go right on the day, this bears out that 'preparation is everything'. One further statistic: when the runner had not achieved 500 miles in the previous six months, 79 per cent did not achieve their target marathon time.

The Schedule

Rule one, as seen above, is 'make haste slowly'. Athletes who have run previously may find the first few weeks too easy and too slow; however, if you are in any doubt at all, start here. Only if you are totally confident that you have already done the base training required should you skip

---

SCHEDULE WEEKS 1 TO 6

Week 1

Monday	Tuesday	Wednesday	Thursday	Friday	Saturday	Sunday
walk 15min	rest	walk 15min	rest	walk 15min	rest	walk 5min

Week 2

Monday	Tuesday	Wednesday	Thursday	Friday	Saturday	Sunday
rest	walk 20min	rest	walk 20min	rest	walk 20min	rest

Week 3

Monday	Tuesday	Wednesday	Thursday	Friday	Saturday	Sunday
walk 20min	walk 20min	rest	walk 20min	rest	walk 25min	rest

Week 4 introduces the first run, 5min only.

Week 4

Monday	Tuesday	Wednesday	Thursday	Friday	Saturday	Sunday
walk 15min run 5min	walk 20min	rest	walk 20min	rest	walk 25min	rest

Week 5

Monday	Tuesday	Wednesday	Thursday	Friday	Saturday	Sunday
rest	walk 10min run 10min	rest	walk 20min	rest	walk 20min run 5min	rest

Week 6

Monday	Tuesday	Wednesday	Thursday	Friday	Saturday	Sunday
walk 15min run 15min	walk 20min	rest	walk 10min run 10min	rest	walk 25min	rest

these six weeks' introduction. Running is gradually introduced from week four and builds up as walking time drops off. For this initial training schedule, running should feel comfortable and pace is not important. This training schedule is designed to finish a half- or full marathon. To improve your finishing time, you should look at Chapter 7. The training schedule can be used for both a half- and full marathon. The half-marathon is programmed for the end of week 30, the full marathon at the end of week 36.

Important! If the intention is to train for a half-marathon, then the times set out in week 30 should be halved.

Weeks 1 to 6

The first six weeks have only a total of 45min of running, and this doesn't start until week 4 with just 5min! This build-up period of almost all walking, allows the bones to become accustomed to the new stresses of training and impact; it also gives an 'early warning' period of time to see if there are any medical aspects to consider.

Weeks 7 to 12

During this training period, where the running time is doubled from 25 to 50min, each week it is very possible that some muscle soreness in the legs, and some indications of discomfort and possible injury, may appear. However easy the athlete may have considered the previous six weeks of 'walking' training, this soreness and discomfort are indications that training was too stressful and demanding. If this does occur, back off! Trying to train through the pain will lead to more severe injury in the future and the likelihood of needing to take a long time away from running.

SCHEDULE WEEKS 7 TO 12

Week 7

Monday	Tuesday	Wednesday	Thursday	Friday	Saturday	Sunday
walk 15min run 15min	walk 25min	rest	walk 10min run 10min	rest	walk 25min run 5min	rest

Week 8

Monday	Tuesday	Wednesday	Thursday	Friday	Saturday	Sunday
walk 15min run 15min	walk 25min	rest	walk 15min run 10min	rest	walk 25min run 5min	rest

Week 9

Monday	Tuesday	Wednesday	Thursday	Friday	Saturday	Sunday
walk 15min run 15min	walk 10min run 5min	rest	walk 15min run 10min	walk 25min run 5min	rest	walk 20min

Week 10

Monday	Tuesday	Wednesday	Thursday	Friday	Saturday	Sunday
walk 15min run 15min	walk 10min run 10min	rest	run 15min	walk 25min run 5min	rest	walk 20min

Week 11

Monday	Tuesday	Wednesday	Thursday	Friday	Saturday	Sunday
walk 15min run 15min	walk 10min run 10min	rest	walk 15min run 15min	walk 25min run 5min	rest	walk 20min

Week 12

Monday	Tuesday	Wednesday	Thursday	Friday	Saturday	Sunday
walk 15min run 15min	walk 10min run 10min	rest	walk 15min run 15min	rest	walk 25min run 10min	rest

Any time of day, early or late running.

It doesn't have to be flat.

Running alone.

Weeks 13 to 18

These six weeks are when 'real' running training begins. From a week of half-and-half walking and running, we progress to all-running time. Running training time builds from 1h up to 2h.

SCHEDULE WEEKS 13 TO 18

Week 13

Monday	Tuesday	Wednesday	Thursday	Friday	Saturday	Sunday
walk 15min	walk 10min	rest	walk 15min	rest	walk 10min	rest
run 15min	run 10min		run 15min		run 20min	

Week 14

Monday	Tuesday	Wednesday	Thursday	Friday	Saturday	Sunday
walk 10min	walk 10min	rest	walk 15min	rest	walk 10min	rest
run 20min	run 10min		run 20min		run 20min	

Week 15

Monday	Tuesday	Wednesday	Thursday	Friday	Saturday	Sunday
walk 10min	walk 5min	rest	walk 10min	rest	walk 5min	rest
run 25min	run 20min		run 25min		run 20min	

Week 16

Monday	Tuesday	Wednesday	Thursday	Friday	Saturday	Sunday
run 30min	rest	walk 5min	walk 5min	rest	run 25min	rest
		run 20min	run 25min			

Week 17

Monday	Tuesday	Wednesday	Thursday	Friday	Saturday	Sunday
run 30min	rest	run 35min	walk 10min	rest	run 25min	rest
			run 20min			

Week 18

Monday	Tuesday	Wednesday	Thursday	Friday	Saturday	Sunday
run 30min	rest	run 40min	run 20min	rest	run 30min	rest

Weeks 19 to 24

This period is a further build-up of running hours and miles and a consolidation of the previous six weeks particularly. Also incorporated is a slight recovery week (week 24) and a first race or time trial at the end of that week of 6 miles or 10,000m. This is to review how the training has progressed and also to give some indication of what might be expected for a half-marathon (in a further 6 weeks' time) and the marathon in 12 weeks' time. Running time for week 23 is up to 3h and then there is a slight drop in running time to take account for both recovery and the race in the following week.

SCHEDULE WEEKS 19 TO 24

Week 19

Monday	Tuesday	Wednesday	Thursday	Friday	Saturday	Sunday
run 30min	rest	run 40min	run 30min	rest	run 40min	run 20min

Week 20

Consolidation – exactly as last week.

Monday	Tuesday	Wednesday	Thursday	Friday	Saturday	Sunday
run 30min	rest	run 40min	run 30min	rest	run 40min	run 20min

Week 21

Monday	Tuesday	Wednesday	Thursday	Friday	Saturday	Sunday
run 30min	rest	run 40min	run 30min	rest	run 40min	run 30min

Week 22

Consolidation – exactly as last week.

Monday	Tuesday	Wednesday	Thursday	Friday	Saturday	Sunday
run 30min	rest	run 40min	run 30min	rest	run 40min	run 30min

Week 23

Monday	Tuesday	Wednesday	Thursday	Friday	Saturday	Sunday
run 45min	rest	run 30min	run 45min	rest	run 30min	run 30min

Week 24

Monday	Tuesday	Wednesday	Thursday	Friday	Saturday	Sunday
run 45min	rest	run 30min	run 45min	rest	rest	run (6 mile or 10,000m race)

Weeks 25 to 30

With just 12 weeks to go to the marathon at the start of this 6-week period, three things become important:

- building up weekly running time,
- increasing the number of days of running,
- the time of one or more individual long runs.

Week 25 should be treated gently, as you will be recovering from that first race. A half-marathon race or time trial of 13 miles should be scheduled in at the end of week 30; there will only be 6 weeks remaining!

Congratulations! You are a half-marathon runner!

Now is the time to rest and recuperate … or, if you've planned it, to carry on with the next six weeks to complete your training for the full marathon and to run it.

SCHEDULE WEEKS 25 TO 30

Week 25

Monday	Tuesday	Wednesday	Thursday	Friday	Saturday	Sunday
run 20min	rest	run 45min	run 45min	rest	run 60min	run 30min

Week 26

Monday	Tuesday	Wednesday	Thursday	Friday	Saturday	Sunday
run 30min	rest	run 45min	run 45min	rest	run 60min	run 30min

Week 27

Monday	Tuesday	Wednesday	Thursday	Friday	Saturday	Sunday
run 30min	rest	run 60min	run 45min	rest	run 60min	run 30min

Week 28

Monday	Tuesday	Wednesday	Thursday	Friday	Saturday	Sunday
run 60min	run 30min	run 45min	run 45min	rest	run 90min	run 30min

Week 29

Monday	Tuesday	Wednesday	Thursday	Friday	Saturday	Sunday
run 60min	run 30min	run 60min	run 45min	rest	run 90min	run 30min

Week 30

Monday	Tuesday	Wednesday	Thursday	Friday	Saturday	Sunday
run 60min	run 45min	rest	run 60min	run 45min	rest	run race (half-marathon or 13-mile time trial)

Weeks 31 to 36

Week 31 will need a slight easing off to recover from that first half-marathon. Weeks 32 to 34 will be the biggest mileage and time, while week 35 will require a slight easing off, and the final week, going into the marathon race, a big cutback on training to allow the body to rest, recover and prepare for the race. There will be an increasing distance long run each week, and a minimum of six days' training each week (except for the final week's preparation). **Congratulations!** You are a marathon runner!

There you are, you've done it! All those weeks of training, the sore legs, the aches and pains, the time on your feet, perhaps out in the cold. But it was worth it, you can now call yourself a marathon runner. Perhaps you can be tempted now to look at your training further, and see what you can do with a mixture of comprehensive training to include much more than pure time on your feet and building up mileage.

SCHEDULE WEEKS 31 TO 36

Week 31

Monday	Tuesday	Wednesday	Thursday	Friday	Saturday	Sunday
run 30min	run 30min	run 90min	run 45min	rest	run 60min	run 120min

Week 32

Monday	Tuesday	Wednesday	Thursday	Friday	Saturday	Sunday
rest	run 90min	run 45min	run 90min	run 60min	run 45min	run 120min

Week 33

Monday	Tuesday	Wednesday	Thursday	Friday	Saturday	Sunday
rest	run 90min	run 45min	run 90min	run 60min	run 45min	run 150min

Week 34

Monday	Tuesday	Wednesday	Thursday	Friday	Saturday	Sunday
rest	run 90min	run 45min	run 90min	run 60min	run 45min	run 150–165min

Week 35

Monday	Tuesday	Wednesday	Thursday	Friday	Saturday	Sunday
rest	run 90min	run 45min	run 90min	run 60min	run 45min	run 60min

Week 36

Monday	Tuesday	Wednesday	Thursday	Friday	Saturday	Sunday
rest	run 60min	rest	run 45min	rest	run 15min	race (marathon)

CHAPTER 7

ADVANCED TRAINING

When you have finished your first marathon or half-marathon and made that decision to continue on to your next one, the target becomes not just finishing, but the time that you finish in. Long, slow, distance running by itself will no longer be enough and it is time to look at a more comprehensive training programme. This will be a programme that still incorporates endurance, but will also use repetition and interval training faster than your half- or full-marathon pace and also some strength (usually hill running) and speed work. Improvements in time in all distances below half- and full marathon will improve that finishing time – provided you maintain the endurance-type running.

Set a Target

The initial aim is to set out your target time. Base it on your finishing time for your first half- or full marathon but also use the

---

SETTING A TARGET TIME

So what will that target time be? Let's have a look at the pace per mile required. A running pace of:

- 6min/mile will give a half-marathon time of 1h, 18min
- 7min/mile will give a half-marathon time of 1h, 31min
- 8min/mile will give a half-marathon time of 1h, 45min
- 9min/mile will give a half-marathon time of 1h, 58min
- 10min/mile will give a half-marathon time of 2h, 11min
- 6min/mile will give a marathon time of 2h, 37min
- 7min/mile will give a marathon time of 3h, 3min
- 8min/mile will give a marathon time of 3h, 30min
- 9min/mile will give a marathon time of 3h, 56min
- 10min/mile will give a marathon time of 4h, 22min.

---

times that you set for the trial 10,000m (and half-marathon race).

Be absolutely realistic with yourself and base your target on what's already been achieved, plus the time and effort that you will be able to give to training. Can you train three times each week, or every day? Will there be some weeks when you can manage to run twice a day? Will you have adequate time for rest and recovery? Decide and stick to your outline plan. If it soon becomes apparent that your training regime is unrealistic, then change it.

Session One

Step one for this 'target' training is to begin with just over one-third of the half- or full-marathon distance, 5 miles and 9 miles, respectively, and run this distance at your target speed: 30, 35, 40, 45 or 50min for half-marathon; and 54, 63, 72, 81 or 90min for full marathon. During the initial starting phase of training run this 5- or 9-mile distance once a week until you can hit this target speed, not once but for two weeks in succession. This will minimize the chance of a 'freak' week. When you have run the two sets of 5 or 9 miles, it is time to move up just 1 mile in distance to 6 miles or 10 miles and maintain that pace, now giving us 6-mile times of 36, 42, 48, 54, 60min and 10-mile times of 60, 70, 80, 90 and 100min.

This single aspect of training should be continued up to runs of around 10 miles and 18 miles, two-thirds of half- and full-marathon distance. Do not assume that

The long run is always essential for training.

progression will be consistent and constant, there will be hiccups and plateaus when no improvement seems to be made for some time, and then there will be a big step forward. Runners and coaches refer to this as the 'staircase effect' – an improvement followed by a period of time when performance remains the same, or may even fall off slightly.

Session Two

Step two is to attempt one long run each week (preferably) when you are running for the same amount of time as your target marathon time. This does not mean that you are racing a marathon each week! Add 1min (at least) to your mile pace and run at this speed, which should feel relatively relaxed. The aim and idea is to know what it feels like to be running for half- and full-marathon racing times.

So, if your aim is a 90min half-marathon (just faster than 7min/mile pace), then you must aim to be able to complete 90min without stopping, running at 8min/mile pace pace, a total of just over 11 miles.

Similarly, if your aim is a 3h marathon (again just faster than 7min/mile pace), then you must aim to be able to complete 3h without stopping, running at 8min/mile pace, a total of 22½ miles.

The step-one and step-two sessions above are the basic endurance sessions, very similar to those that you will have worked up to in your initial training. It is essential that you continue these while you add in the faster, more quality-type training sessions.

Faster Pace Sessions

We have looked at racing other distances and also comparison times for all distances up to a marathon in this book. To be able to run a good half-marathon or marathon it is critical that we do some quality training that is comparable to these race speeds. It is important to train and, if possible, to race at 10 and 5km, 3000 and 1500m pace in addition to the endurance runs. Be careful not to 'over-race' (race too frequently), as this will tire you too much and leave you feeling permanently exhausted. Perhaps setting out a race schedule of once a month up to the half- or full marathon, starting with 3km then 5km, 10km, 10 miles and half-marathon (only if aiming for a full marathon), one month apart, will maintain your speed, gradually increase the racing distance and prepare you for the next half- or full marathon. Remember that your (half-) marathon pace will not be as fast as any of these races, so it should make you mentally strong when you start the next (half-) marathon.

The freedom to run anywhere makes training pleasant, even when tough!

Timed interval and repetition running is essential.

Interval Training

When you first begin to train at speeds faster than race pace, the intensity will make you extremely tired. Interval training is the real hard work of training, where big improvements can be made. The basic principles behind interval training are these:

- You run fast for a period of time to gain speed.
- You repeat the effort a number of times to gain endurance.
- The shorter the effort and the longer the resting interval, the more your speed will improve.
- The longer the effort and the shorter the resting interval, the more your endurance will improve.
- Interval training can be extremely demanding and tiring.
- Interval training carried out properly leads to big improvements.
- A critical factor in training for a half- and for a full marathon is the resting/recovery interval between efforts; too long a recovery period may lead to an improvement in speed but this will not be relevant to half- and full marathon running.

Repetition Training

Interval and repetition training have become mixed up and, although there is no rigid dividing line between them, interval training usually has a fairly short rest between the efforts, whereas repetition training will have a considerably longer rest but will require that the efforts are carried out at a much higher speed and intensity. Repetition training is more often appropriate for 400, 800 and 1500m runners, than for distance athletes.

Speedwork is important, even for marathon and half-marathon.

INTERVAL TRAINING SESSION

An example of an interval training session might be:

6 × 800m with a 200m jog recovery in 60sec.

A repetition training session might be:

3 × 800m with 10min recovery

Speedwork is an integral part of successful running.

THE DIRT PRINCIPLE

Let us start with a fairly simple training session: four repetitions of 1 mile to be completed in 6min each, with a resting interval of 4min between each repetition:

- Distance to be run: 1 mile.
- Interval between effort: 4min.
- Repetitions: 3.
- Time for each effort: 6min.

Any of the DIRT factors can be improved by increasing or reducing the number involved:

- We can increase the number of repetitions.
- We can increase the distance of the repetitions.
- We can decrease the resting time between the repetitions.
- We can decrease the time taken for completing the repetitions.

1st increase:
- Distance: 1 mile.
- Interval: 4min.
- Repetitions: 4.
- Time: 6min.

2nd increase:
- Distance: 1 mile.
- Interval: 3min.
- Repetitions: 4.
- Time: 6min.

3rd increase:
- Distance: 1 mile.
- Interval: 3min.
- Repetitions: 4.
- Time: 5 min.

4th increase:
Distance: 2000m.
- Interval: 3min.
- Repetitions: 4.
- Time: 7min, 5sec (the pace for each 400m is 5sec faster).

Background to Interval Training

Three running coaches are often credited with the popularity of interval training: Franz Stampfl, Mihlov Igloi and Woldemar Gerschler, all of whom had remarkable success with their particular brand of interval/repetition training, including the first 4min mile, Olympic Gold medals and World Records.

There is little doubt that the phenomenal improvements seen in running times from National to World level over the last 50 to 60 years have been because of the extensive use of interval training in one form or another. Running legend Emil Zatopek had a favourite running session of:

20 × 200m, followed by 20 × 400m, followed by a further 20 × 200m,

all with a short-jog recovery of half the running distance. The total of the 'hard' running is 10 miles, plus the jog recovery, warm up and warm down, 16 to 19 miles, no wonder that the man was unbeatable at his peak. Previous World 10,000m champion Liz McColgan has a session of 10 sets of 1-mile repeats, each run in 5min with just 30sec recovery. (This session totals 10 miles in 54min 30sec, including the recovery period.)

Start Slowly!

To attempt to run your early interval training sessions like Zatopek or McColgan would clearly be ridiculous and would certainly lead to injury. It is important to start (as we did in the 'basic training') easily and gradually build up to harder and more demanding sessions. This is based on the DIRT principle (see box, left).

Using any one of these increases as you become fitter will lead to even better running times. However, do not be tempted to try to make the increases too frequently or to combine two or more increases at the same time. If one step is taken every 2 weeks, then over a 6-month period there will be twelve improvements (three each of the DIRT factors) made in the severity of training. Our initial session above could then look like this:

- Distance to be run: 2,400m (1½ miles).
- Interval between effort: 90sec.
- Repetitions: 6.

Training with a partner or group makes things more pleasant.

- Time for each effort: 7½min (5min/mile pace).

A significant improvement!

10km-Pace Training

If you are fairly new to interval and multi-pace training, it is important to find a starting point. This schedule (in a variety of forms) has been used with great success by many 5,000m, 10,000m, half- and full-marathon runners. To find the starting point for your 10km-speed training, run for 15min as hard as you can (preferably on a running track) and take the exact distance covered (for simplicity, we will say 3,000m). Then follow the 10km specific programme.

A further example of improving a 'starting' session for a fast runner would be to aim for 12 × 800m in 2min 24sec with 90sec recovery. Once this is achieved, the next target building on this is 10 × 1,000m in 3min (the same pace but distance increased) still with 90sec recovery.

THE 10km PROGRAMME

1 Run twice the distance (6,000m) in double the time plus 10 per cent/3min (33min). Aim to reduce this by 1min every 6 weeks. This session should be done twice within each phase of training.
2 Run half the distance (1,500m) in 7min 30sec (7.30) with 1min rest between the three efforts. You may find that you need to take more rest to begin with. Aim to reduce the time or increase the distance by 15–20sec or 70–100m every 6 weeks.
3 Find 400m pace from the timed run (2min for each 400m.) Halve this (60sec) and take off another 8sec to find 200m pace (52sec). Run a series of 200m in 52sec with reducing recovery. Start at 90sec, then 75, 60, 45, 30, 15sec; start again at 90sec and keep going until you can't maintain 52sec pace. If you feel you can run for ever, then you need to set a faster target; if you run out of speed too quickly and can't do more than seven repetitions, then drop your target time by 2sec. When you can run nineteen repetitions of the 200m (going through the reducing recovery three times), it is time to set a faster target pace.
4 Run over distance. (As you are training overall for a half- or full marathon, this session is already accounted for in your general training programme as session one and/or two; see beginning of this chapter). Start at 6 miles plus a third (8 miles) and gradually work up to double the distance (12 miles). Do not run hard.
5 Hills/resistance and strength work. Run 10km with half of the distance (5km) up hills. If this is not possible, do hill repetitions. Work hard on the hills and jog the recovery.

With two runs being done on session one, there are six sessions in all before the phase is repeated. For example, if the athlete runs three times each week, the entire programme is repeated three times before re-testing is done at the end of a 6-week period.

These six sessions will form the basis of your 10km-pace/speed training. However, don't think that these are the only sessions that you should do for 10km; there are a variety of variations that can be used starting with the sessions above. The 3 × 1,500m interval session may become 4, 5 or 6 × 1,500m as you progress, or if you change the distance factor, 3 × 2,000m and then 3 × 3,000m as you become fitter and more used to this type of training.

EXAMPLES OF FASTER TRAINING

• 5,000m-pace training: 4 × 1,500m with 60sec-jog recovery.
• 3,000m-pace training: 5 × 800m with 90sec-jog recovery.
• 1,500m-pace training: 8 × 400m with 90sec-jog recovery.
• 800m-pace training: 8 × 200m with 90sec-jog recovery.

The aim with the fast sessions listed is to improve the average times of the repetitions.

Gradually increasing the distance of the repetitions, while holding the recovery constant, will eventually give us the target time for 10km.

Faster Running and Training

Just as it is important to run at 10km pace to improve your half- and full-marathon time and performance, so it is equally important to train at 5,000m, 3,000m and even 1,500 and 800m pace to improve the performance of the distance above each one. Training at a faster-than-race-pace speed will develop better economy of effort, timing and coordination, and comfort while running fast. So, to achieve a good 10k time, the athlete has to bring the 5k time down; to run a good 5k, you'll need to bring the 3,000m time down and equally the 1,500m time as well.

Judging Training Pace

To do this, you will have to train at racing pace for these distances; the pace/time differences will vary with each runner and their level of fitness, but as a very

Using other runners as motivation to run faster.

LEFT: Finishing a training session can be pure relief!

BELOW: Taking part in shorter road races is an integral part of your training.

Variable-Pace Sessions

In addition to specific training sessions at one particular pace of running, there are a number of sessions that combine the training pace between marathon or half-marathon or 10km pace, and faster. These variable paces have proved to be particularly effective when runners have reached a plateau and seem unable to improve, and also with experienced distance runners. Importantly, the slowest efforts are at target marathon/half-marathon/10km pace.

Session One: 5km/Marathon Pace

Continuous 400m efforts are run at target 5km time, and target marathon time. An experienced runner with a best 5km time of 19min and a target marathon time of

general rule of thumb, this will be about 5sec less for each 400m as you go down each distance. The time for each 400m at 5000m-pace training will be 5sec faster than that at 10,000m-pace training. The time for each 400m at 3,000m-pace training will be 5sec less than that at 5,000m pace and so on.

3h would aim to run consecutive 400m efforts at 90sec and 1min, 45sec. The aim would be to run 25 (or more) consecutive 400m.

In shorthand:

25 × 400m alternating 1.30/1.45.

This gives a total of 10km with more than half of this distance, and therefore more than the 5km distance at 5km racing pace. Being able to run the full 10km will depend on fitness. If the runner is not yet fit enough to do the full distance, then split into two (or more) sets of 400m, perhaps 16 × 400m then 9 × 400m with a short recovery in between.

Session Two: Mixed-Pace Speed Session

After a warm-up, 10min is run at best 5km pace, followed by a 3min-jog recovery. The runner then goes straight into ten sets of 30sec effort at 800m pace with a 30sec-

Effort during training; sessions can be anywhere.

jog recovery only in between, followed by a further 3min-jog recovery. The runner then goes into the final set of a 1min, 2min and 3min effort at best 1,500m pace with just 1min-jog recovery in between.

In shorthand:

- 10min at 5km pace, 3min-jog recovery.
- 10 × 30sec at 800m pace, 30sec jog, 3min-jog recovery.
- 1, 2, 3min at 1,500m pace with 1min-jog recovery only.

Session Three: Multiple-Pace Session

This session, sometimes called 'acceleration' session, has been used (with variations) by previous women's 10,000m World Champions and the Women's Marathon World Record Holder. When starting to use this demanding session, no running is slower than marathon-race pace; and after initial training, no running is slower than 10,000m-race pace. The example shown is geared at no slower than 10,000m pace:

- run 400m at current 5km-race pace
  straight into:
- run 400m at 10km-race pace
  straight into:
- run 300m at 3000m-race pace
  straight into:
- run 300m at 10km-race pace
  straight into:
- run 200m at 1,500m-race pace
  straight into:
- run 200m at 10km-race pace
  straight into:
- run 100m at 800m-race pace (99 per cent effort)
  straight into:
- run 100m at 10km-race pace,
- then repeat this sequence twice more (three times in total).

For experienced athletes, this sequence would be repeated (after a short-jog recovery) twice.

For very experienced athletes, this sequence would be repeated (after a short-jog recovery) just once more.

Total training distances are 6km or 10km or 12km.

Runners with a good background of training may wish to take the session one stage further by four, three, two and one set, ten in total rather than three, two and one set, six in total. This would give a total training distance of 20km, almost the half-marathon distance and double the 10km distance at no slower than 10km-race pace throughout.

The rationale behind this session is that you run faster and faster throughout the session. The first set is fine, you feel OK; the second and third time you are more fatigued but you still have to accelerate, even though the recovery jogs are shorter each time. Importantly, each time you restart the 400m effort, you have only had 100m-jog recovery after a hard series of efforts. You get used to running faster when you are tired. Experienced male runners should complete this full set of 12km running in about 45min – including recoveries; experienced female runners in under 50min.

Session Four: Interval Plus Sustained Effort

This session has been used by Ironman Women's World Champion Chrissie Wellington. After the warm-up, 800m is run at 3km/5km pace with a 200m-jog as the resting interval, this is repeated fifteen times. Immediately after the fifteenth repetition, the athlete goes into a hard 3-mile run finishing with a final 800m uphill.

In shorthand:

15 × 800m at 3km/5km pace, 200m-jog recovery, 3-mile run hard.

The total distance of this session is approximately 13 miles (half-marathon) with substantially more than half the distance at faster than half-marathon pace.

Tethered running ... attention to technique is always important.

Three further considerations are:

1   The need for training on hills, either on hilly runs or interval training on hills.
2   A decision to train twice on some days.
3   Recovery runs.

This takes no account of rest days and is geared, perhaps, more towards distance than speed at the shorter distances. It is only an example, and runners must use their own self-knowledge to design their own schedule, and to take advice from coaches and more experienced runners. Perhaps with the addition of rest days from training and more recovery runs, this schedule example could be used on a three-week turnaround basis.

Building a Schedule

To read all the above, you would think you need a mathematics degree to work out your training schedule! Certainly, it takes a lot of thinking out and honesty about acknowledging your strengths and weaknesses. If your endurance is good but your speed less so, then speed training is necessary. Vice versa, if you have speed but need more distance and endurance training your training schedule must reflect that. The necessities are:

1   The long, steady run, time on feet to equal (half-) marathon time target but not at (half-) marathon-racing pace.
2   Marathon- and half-marathon race pace (start at 9 or 5 miles and build up).
3   10,000m-pace session.
4   5,000m-pace session.
5   3,000m-pace session.
6   1,500m-pace session.
7   800m-pace session.
8   Mixed-pace sessions (these may be in addition to the specific pace sessions or as a substitute for them).

A POSSIBLE TRAINING SCHEDULE FOR THE MARATHON

This is a suggestion only! Adjust for your strengths and weaknesses, for your available training days and amount of time, for your running background, for your own knowledge of the likelihood of you getting injured, your recovery from hard training sessions.

1   Long run, slower than marathon pace.
2   5km-pace session.
3   Recovery run, 30 to 40min.
4   Marathon-pace session.
5   1,500m-pace session.
6   Variable-pace session.
7   Recovery run, 30 to 40min.
8   10km-pace session.
9   Hill session.
10   800m-pace session.
11   Long run, slower than marathon pace.
12   5km-pace session.
13   3000m-pace session.
14   Recovery run.
15   Marathon-pace session.
16   10km-pace session.
17   Variable-pace session.
18   Hill session.

CHAPTER 8

RACING AND PACING

Race-day conditions, including road surface, the camber of the road, hills, wind, weather, even the height above sea-level, will all have an effect on race pacing.

Course Factors

A smooth road surface will create much less drag than running on soft surfaces (grass, sand). A flat race will take much less effort than a hilly one; the extra effort and energy used in running up a hill will not be paid back when running downhill. Calm weather conditions with no wind will make running easier than running in windy conditions, even if the race course is out and back or circular; much more energy is used running into wind and this will not be given back when running with the wind at your back. Extreme hot or cold conditions will have a significant impact on running speed, while running at altitude will slow down marathon and

ABOVE: *Be aware of hot conditions and use sun block.*

RIGHT: *Although perhaps not as much as this athlete!*

Using Other Competitors

Other things to consider are running behind or in a pack of runners (drafting) – this will break the effects of a strong wind hitting you in the body and face and even the aerodynamic effect of loose clothing. Although loose clothing may not have a big effect on times, certainly judicious drafting can help, not only by running behind someone to lessen the effects into the wind, but perhaps more importantly, running with someone of a similar standard, who is confident of running at a particular pace, can help you by not going out too slowly or too quickly. For instance, when I ran in the Wolverhampton Marathon many years ago, I stood on the start line and shouted, 'Anyone running at six-minute-mile pace?' and fortunately for me, an experienced marathon runner said 'yes'. He was tremendous. After the first couple of miles to establish a position, he relentlessly ticked off mile after mile spot-on 6min/mile pace, so that I arrived at the 20-mile mark feeling remarkably

ABOVE: Race conditions like these mean that a fast time is highly unlikely!

BELOW: Mountain marathons are extraordinarily tough.

distance running significantly (not so with short-distance running where the times will be much quicker; this became significant at the 1968 Mexico City Olympic Games, where times were drastically different from those achieved by runners at sea-level).

Use a group to help you with appropriate pacing.

fresh – very dissimilar to some previous efforts! I was able to run a faster pace on the final 6 miles than I had for the initial 20 miles, which was very unusual, and I went on to beat a personal best (PB) time by some 12min.

Even Pacing

However, even taking into account all the above, there is one vitally important rule for both the first-time and the experienced marathon and half-marathon runner: do not start too fast! Even a fraction too fast at the start will mean a significant slowdown in the second half of the race, particularly a full marathon. The benefits of all the training, the long runs and, importantly, the running pace from those trial races of 10km and half-marathon will pay dividends here. You will need to pay attention to two things: how you are feeling, and the time on your watch. It is the juggling of these two that will bring you home in a good time. While the mantra of cyclists racing in a time trial is, 'start flat-out, accelerate in the middle, and sprint home', we runners would be better to say, 'start slowly and ease off'.

Ideally, the entire marathon or half-marathon should be run at an even pace. Even if you are feeling really good during the first half of the race, resist any temptation to speed up – going too fast too early almost certainly means that you will pay for it during the second half of the race.

In my first marathon I was convinced by 'expert' outsiders, who didn't really know my running ability, that I could run a 2h, 32min marathon when I had estimated 2.45 to 2.50. They were very persuasive! Armed with their words and misplaced confidence, I committed the classic mistake of going out too fast. I reached the halfway point in 74min (my best half-marathon time ever was 72min) and felt fine, I was flying! Within the next three miles I paid the price, by 16 miles I was struggling and the final ten miles were not a happy experience. I finished well outside my 2.50 estimated time with the second half taking 99min, a slowing down of some 25min, almost 2min/mile! Had I had the experience

ABOVE: *For efficient pacing, don't go off too fast at the start.*

BELOW: *Running by yourself in a race takes self-confidence to know that you're pacing properly.*

and confidence not to go too fast, my first marathon would have been a much happier experience and I would have achieved a considerably faster finishing time.

Even-paced running does not mean even-paced effort; fatigue and tiredness mean that you will have to work progressively harder to maintain the same pace.

Experienced, top-class marathon runners will have the ability, through their knowledge of distance running, of knowing to within a very few seconds just how fast they are running; at that top level, where tactics will come into play as the race draws on, this is invaluable. Again, on a personal level, my slower, even pacing at the Wolverhampton Marathon meant that I was able to run the second half faster than the first.

Sections and Checking

Despite all and any advice on correct, even pace racing, it is still very easy to start too fast. The excitement and euphoria (particularly if it is a first attempt at the marathon) of being at the start, the other runners all around you, the count-down to the start, the queuing and re-queuing for the portaloos, even that particular smell of other runners with Vaseline, liniment and talcum powder, can all serve to set you off too fast. Check your pace early. Start your watch as you cross the line and as soon as you have run one mile (there will be markers right along

Training alone and ensuring that you know your exact pace will ensure that you don't run too fast too early during a race.

If you do find yourself running alone, perhaps in the smaller races, a knowledge of pacing is very important.

the course and any reputable marathon), look at your elapsed time – more often than not, you will have started too fast. Adjust your pace, and if it feels too slow and that you have too much energy, that's fine! All that energy will be more than useful in the final few miles. Keep checking your pace with every mile and get into the pace that you decided upon. For many first-time marathoners, this is the only way to check pace.

Pack Running

As the race progresses, you will find yourself in a loose group of runners who are all (obviously) running the same pace as you are. This may be the time to talk and see if there is an experienced runner in your group who knows that he will be able to maintain the same pace throughout the race. If so, trust him and run alongside or just behind. Keep checking your watch so you can check his pace-judgement, as well as your own.

Packs will quickly form during a race and help your race pace speed, if it is the right pack for you.

Hydration

Drink early – if you're thirsty, then you have left it too late. You will need to drink throughout the race as fluid absorption is constant and is unable to make up for time lost. Water will be available at drinking stations on the course. Ensure that you know where these are by reading the race literature or listening to the race briefing before the race. Some marathoners prefer to drink the glucose, sugary type of drinks. You must try these out in training before the race; just as you wouldn't wear a brand new pair of running shoes, don't try out a new drink. Different runners are affected in different ways and new drinks should not be tried for the first time during a race. Do not drink iced or very cold water as this too may upset your stomach.

FAR RIGHT: Make sure you have adequate hydration by taking on water early.

Association and Disassociation

For the first few miles you will be concentrating on your race. Being aware of pacing, of runners very close around you, runners brushing past you and you passing other runners will take all your attention; this total concentration is called association. However, as the race progresses, perhaps by the 5- or 6-mile mark, the field will thin out and your thoughts may drift to other things rather than purely on the race itself. This disassociation can be helpful as it can make the race pass more quickly. You will pass the 12-mile mark (in a full marathon) and think, 'Where did the last three miles go?' The downside of disassociation can be that if your thoughts drift off too much, you may lose control of your pace. Some experienced marathon runners consider the first four or five miles are association as they get themselves established into the leading pack, then a long mid-section

Even in wet conditions, you must take on water!

of the race, perhaps up to twenty miles, where they are aware of the runners around them but are content to maintain their place in the pack, and then the final six miles where it becomes total association as individual runners will try to speed up or break away and will need to be immediately covered.

Making that decision to walk or not to walk …

Stay With It

Unless there is something medically wrong or you become ill or injured during the race, try not to drop out. However, if you do feel ill, drop out immediately.

Similarly, you should have a plan about walking. If you have trained and prepared properly with lots of long runs, then there shouldn't be the need to walk. However, if there have been reasons why you haven't been able to do everything that you set yourself for training, then be realistic and allow yourself to walk. Have a plan for this; mix walking with running, rather than exhausting yourself early on and being forced to walk the final four or six or eight miles. Perhaps run but walk through the water and drink stations. If they're situated every three miles, you will be running eight to nine lots of three miles with a short recovery in between. Maybe run a mile and then walk 100 paces. Do have a plan and try to stick to it.

If you have chosen a marathon or half-marathon with hills, be aware that the energy cost of running up hills is far more than on the flat. One formula used is that a 1 per cent slope requires 5 per cent more energy to maintain the same speed. You will not be able to make all of this up on the downhill section. Particularly steep downhills will require attention and can be very painful on the legs.

You may need to go to the toilet during the race. Be prepared. Carry some toilet paper with you. If you are forced to stop, don't try to make up the lost time immediately.

The Wall – Hit or Miss?

Runners talk about 'hitting the wall' during the marathon. What happens is that, at around the 20-mile mark, most of the available energy from carbohydrates will have been used up and your body begins to take more energy from fat (see Chapter 10). As this takes a little time to process, your body and mind need to dig deep to keep going. Some runners say that the marathon really begins at the 20-mile point. Runners have experimented with special diets (the carbohydrate bleed-out diet particularly) to try to avoid this. Some runners never have any problem, apart from the extreme fatigue that they are expecting. Certainly there have been many runners who have suffered badly during those last six miles, as well as many runners who suffer no more than in the previous twenty. If you're having a 'bad' race, then mentally the final few miles will hurt. Conversely, if you're running well and enjoying the experience, the final few miles can be the best of the whole race. Hitting the 'wall' is unlikely to be experienced during a half-marathon.

Judging Pace from Other Distances

It is possible to get very accurate estimated pace times from racing at other distances, particularly 10km and half-marathons (see Chapter 15). These comparison times work better with experienced runners and will only be accurate if marathon training has been consistent. In short, don't expect that a good 10km race time will automatically give a good marathon or half-marathon time, unless a proper training plan to include long training runs has been done.

BELOW: Running on sand during competition or training will have a huge effect on speed and pacing.

RIGHT: Hills and inclines can make a significant difference to race pace and finishing times.

CHAPTER 9

MENTAL ATTITUDE

The most important muscle is the mind.

A cliché, but clichés become just that because they're true!

As sport generally, and running particularly, has developed along professional lines more and more in the last twenty years, so it has become more and more important to focus on the extra attributes that will provide an edge. It is self-evident that runners of a similar standard will have similar standards of fitness and physical ability. Why then, does one athlete usually beat another, although they are both similarly fit and similarly physically prepared? Perhaps it is because that winning athlete believes that he or she will win. It is a crucial belief and attitude to have – a strong

mental attitude. It is important to train mental attitude just as we train physically; we become physically fitter by physical training, therefore we become mentally fitter by mental training.

The importance of mental attitude and sports psychology has become more appreciated but, although its importance is realized, it is surprising how few athletes carry this out in practice. It is almost as if sports psychology is important for world-class runners but not for everyday athletes. This is untrue. Perhaps one reason is that non-professional athletes and coaches fear that they do not know as much about mental training as physical training and back away from it. If we compare this with the physical training required for distance

running, it is accepted that 'train to your weaknesses, race to your strengths' is a base to training. Similarly if current training of mental attitude is weak, then emphasis should be put on that part of training. Certainly nerves can play a great part in determining how well an athlete will perform in a race, but an understanding of why nervousness becomes greater may well help, rather than hinder, an athlete. Sports psychologists talk about 'level of arousal'. In everyday terms, this is dealing with nerves. All runners will race to their best ability when they are mentally and physically prepared but, while some will want to be relaxed before competition, others will need to be tense for a race. Finding that correct level of arousal is important to compete with the best possible attitude.

There are no children competing in marathons! Distance and marathon runners have chosen to take part, and this is a very positive point, there are no excuses as in 'I didn't want to do this'. Training and racing in distance, half-marathon and marathon running has been the athlete's choice and the level of disillusionment and dropping out is likely to be less. However, there still remains the question of why and how some athletes seem to be able to motivate themselves to maintain pressure when they are extremely tired. It is certainly not just the physical aspects and the training, if it were, then everyone would be able to do it. Knowledge of different types of training methods is shared widely and there are few secrets of training. Yet some athletes always seem to under-achieve while others seem to always over-achieve.

Positive Thoughts

It is absolutely essential that training and racing are approached positively, rather

15-year-old Sky Draper shows intense concentration before a major race.

The joy and relief at finishing first!

Pre-track-race focus and concentration for Faye Harding.

than negatively. Negative thoughts will always lead to poor training and poor racing performances. Worrying about racing, wishing that you didn't have to go training or race a particular event, feelings of letting others down by a poor performance, will all have a negative impact.

The notion of self-belief is very important here, not hoping or thinking that you will have a great race, but actually believing that you will! That confidence or belief is paramount. It is not only a mental attitude. Negative thoughts produce a different physiological reaction from positive thoughts. Distance runners work less efficiently, become fatigued more quickly and actually train and race with less energy than they would with a positive mental attitude.

Winning Characteristics

It is not only self-belief that is important to succeed. There are a number of other important qualities required to achieve full potential in training and in racing. Although these may go by slightly different names, they would include: self-discipline, self-reliance, self-motivation, determination, organization and concentration. Note the importance of 'self' here.

Deeper analysis indicates that these qualities are absolutely necessary to be able to train and race successfully. These include:

- Self-motivation and drive:
  - A desire to win and to be successful.
  - A willingness and aspiration to accomplish and overcome difficulties.
  - Setting high goals and aims.
  - A positive attitude to competition.
  - A desire and need to achieve excellence.

Total concentration before her pole vault for Yelena Isinbayeva.

Great Britain's Christine Ohuruogu takes a quiet moment before the World Championship Final.

- Aggressiveness:
  - A belief that it is sometimes necessary to be aggressive in order to succeed.
  - A willingness to become aggressive and enjoying aspects of confrontation and argument.
  - Can be forceful to ensure that personal points of view are accepted.
  - A refusal to be intimidated and dominated.
  - Will not forget disrespect from others.

- Determination:
  - Willing to train hard for a long time, to work on skill aspects until exhausted and willingness to frequently train alone.
  - Perseverance in training despite inconsistent results.
  - Has a long-term plan and will persist in training and competition to achieve this.

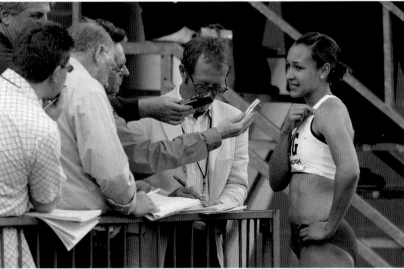

TOP LEFT: In many ways, it doesn't matter what the event is. Strong mental attitude is essential for everything. Here Jessica Ennis celebrates a successful high jump clearance.

ABOVE: For somebody like Jessica Ennis, there is always the need to maintain focus on the race, despite intrusions from the press and autograph hunters.

- Self-analysis:
  - Accepts responsibility for actions, blame and criticism, whatever the circumstances.
  - Examines 'when things go wrong'.
  - Endures physical and mental pain and discomfort, and injury.
- Leadership and self-confidence:
  - Will take control of training sessions and believe that the session is correct and will influence other athletes to conform and join in, often by force of personality.
  - Will make decisions and believe them to be correct.
  - Completely self-confident, including the ability to deal with everything that may occur.
  - Confident in strengths and abilities.

- Emotional control:
  - Emotionally stable and realistic, and not easily upset or put off.
  - Will control emotions in training and racing.
  - Will not allow emotions about negative incidents outside his or her control.
- Tenacity and willingness to be coached:
  - Will accept strong criticism and will not become upset or angry when losing or racing poorly.
  - Durability, the ability to bounce back from adversity.
  - Will accept advice and dominant coaching but does not necessarily invite encouragement from coaches, although respects coaches and the coaching process and considers good coaching essential.
  - Accepts and respects team captains, authorities, race organizers and governing bodies.

Total focus immediately before the event from USA's Sanya Richards.

Yuriy Borzakovskiy immediately before the World Championships 800m final.

- preparing your equipment immaculately for your race or training session leads to
- excellent results in training and racing.

All of these improved mental attitudes and their physical results will almost inevitably bring better race results and training performances. Everything that you have done leads to this – you expect to race well, so you do (self-fulfilling prophecy). This makes you feel even better about yourself, and ensures that the cycle revolves onwards and upwards.

The success cycle undoubtedly works. However, when things go wrong, it can be easy to get stuck in the circle of failure. This starts with a negative self-image and proceeds along similar lines (but with all the negatives) of the success cycle:

- having low expectations of yourself
- expecting yourself to do poorly
- poor training and incorrect lifestyle habits
- eating and drinking poorly
- not sleeping enough
- poor lifestyle habits
- poor preparing of equipment.

Inevitably a poor race result follows (once again a self-fulfilling prophecy) and this negative cycle will continue.

A positive self-image leads to the other positive factors. It becomes very much

- Conscientious:
  - Follow advice, coaching and training schedules and will not make excuses.
  - Will consider running and its training as a major part of his/her life, and will never make excuses.

Along with these characteristics, there are three steps to success:

1 Decide exactly what is wanted. This must be as specific as setting exact times not only for the marathon, but also for each racing distance up to it: 5km, 10km, half-marathon. It will also include knowledge of 'split' times needed during racing and training. Generalities are not sufficient.
2 Exactly what is required to get there, to achieve that specific aim? Again it is essential that this is exact, and every requirement laid out.
3 What is the opportunity cost of these needs? Time taken? Effort needed? Earning opportunities lost? Social activities lost?

Frequently it is the third factor that is the inhibiting one.

The Success Cycle

Mental preparation is essential for full potential to be achieved. The success cycle is based upon starting with a positive self-image and then the remaining attributes below, all leading on to each other:

- a positive self-image leads to
- a positive attitude to running leads to
- having high expectations of yourself leads to
- better training leads to
- better lifestyle habits leads to
- eating and drinking properly and sleeping regularly leads to
- not taking part in activities that have an adverse effect on training leads to

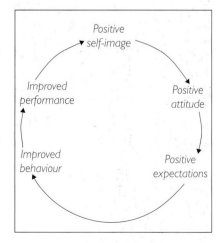

The success cycle.

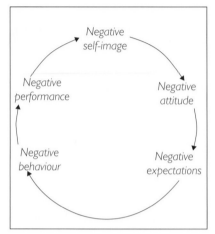

The cycle of failure.

about being in control and taking control, rather than allowing negative aspects to control you. It is very much about feeling good about yourself, and being in control of your life and of your training. It is very much that self-belief that 'I can and I will'. Poor performers are reluctant to take any control and rather allow other factors to control them.

Positive self-image and positive outlook on life are also major contributing factors to other examples of a strong mental attitude. Remembering previous excellent race results and previous excellent training sessions will have a huge impact on future racing and training. That powerful muscle, the brain, impacts upon and controls muscle responses. The motivation of reliving previous excellence and visualizing future events establishes a positive pattern – once again that self-fulfilling prophecy. Be aware of dwelling too deeply on poor race results. Rather, decide what went wrong and decide what to do about it in the future. In this way, you are turning negative experiences into positive ones. Our thoughts always influence our reactions, and the anticipation of a pleasant and positive training session or planned race will ensure that reaction occurs. In general, positive thoughts lead to positive reactions, while negative thoughts will get negative reactions. Part of mental-attitude training should be planned, systematic, conscious and positive thinking. A systematic and positive thought process and analysis can change negative behaviour into positive behaviour.

Positive thoughts can dramatically alter performance, while getting into a pattern of negative thinking will adversely affect performance. However, getting into positive thinking will not happen just by chance; just as physical training builds up over years of repetition, so will mental training. The mind and body learn from repetition and that repetition takes time.

Most successful athletes will have a routine (both physical and mental) before an event. The physical routine may well be their warm-up preparation but they will also have a mental warm-up. Thoughts of, 'I feel calm', 'I want to race', 'I am prepared to work hard', 'I will respond to any situation', 'I fear nobody' will all feature in some guise. There will be an avoidance of negatives, and a focus on positives. A positive mental attitude immediately before a race is necessary to race well.

Visualization is critical – not only seeing yourself doing well in the event, but also bringing in the other senses:

- What does the race sound like?
- Smell like? (can you imagine the smell of the start of the Virgin London Marathon)
- Feel like?

Before an Olympic semi-final, total focus is needed by Felix Sanchez.

It is important to anticipate these sensations, otherwise they may come as an unexpected shock. It is important to be relaxed but also ready to race and to imagine yourself racing well. Pre-race preparation should include all the positive thoughts of how well you have trained and prepared, how well you anticipate doing, and focusing on your race tactics rather than worrying about any other runner. Total focus and concentration on the race are essential. Taking a positive attitude into the race and anticipating doing well will ensure that you do race well.

However, despite all the planning and positive attitudes, sometimes things do go wrong! It is important then to have a plan, to have coping skills. This should not be confused with negative thinking, but rather predicting and preparing for problems and having a strategy for dealing with them. Falling over, hitting a barrier, missing a drinks station, blisters and sores are all things that can happen and athletes should have a plan for dealing with them. Sometimes when things do go wrong, it can almost be a relief (especially if it is in a less important race), as runners can then put into action their prepared plan or coping strategy.

Maintaining a positive attitude whatever happens is critical and directly enhances race performance. Without this attitude, race performance will be poorer than it should. Setting both short- and long-term specific and dream goals, and planning how to achieve these goals, are crucial. The visualization and imagination of fulfilling these goals are also essential. This will ensure that preparation and training, both physical and mental, will be successful. The persistence that you bring to training and its repetition are also essential. There are no short-cuts to success and it can be the thoughts of how long it has taken and how much has had to be given up to ensure that success that will carry you through.

GETTING INTO POSITIVE THINKING

Some sports psychologists use the pass process:

- **P**ositive thoughts and words.
- **A**void negatives: no, never, not.
- **S**imple thoughts and words.
- **S**chedule mental training.

The final moment before an appointment with destiny awaits Christine Ohuruogu.

CHAPTER 10

DIET, NUTRITION AND HYDRATION

There are no heats and finals in a half-marathon or marathon. World best times (currently) for men are just under 1h and just under 2h, 4min for the half-marathon and marathon, respectively, and for women, a little over 10 per cent more. Certainly then, this takes away the necessity of planning eating and drinking between races. However, it makes it even more important that good habits in nutrition and hydration are established for general training and racing.

The amount of training and its intensity are the critical ingredients in determining fitness, and although this fitness will not be significantly enhanced by a good diet, a poor diet will significantly lower that fitness. Proper fuelling will influence fitness and race performance – not only what you eat and drink, but also when you eat and drink is important. A healthy diet provides the body with energy.

The correct racing weight and use of ergogenic aids (such as energy drinks), as well as a possible need to drink and eat during longer events, also need to be considered.

What is a Healthy Diet?

We live in a society where food is abundant. Compared to less than half a century ago, the variety and choice is unparalleled. However, this choice, along with influential advertising, can easily confuse. There may be some call for special needs for the runner but, in general terms, an ordinary healthy diet should be adequate. Too much sugar and salt, saturated fat and alcohol will be detrimental, although no one should completely cut them out.

There is a basic need for energy to fuel the body and an increase in the amount of calories will be necessary for somebody in hard training. New entrants to marathon and half-marathon running (or any endurance sport) will often lose a significant amount of weight – usually body fat – in the early days of training, and because marathon running is a weight-bearing sport, that weight loss in the early days will by itself lead to significant improvements in performance and training times. While the general non-active population may require between 2,000 and 2,500 calories each day, distance runners in serious training may double that requirement.

Carbohydrate is the main supplier of energy and runners may need as much as 60 per cent of their calorie intake from carbohydrates. As much as 20 per cent will come from quality protein and perhaps 20 per cent from fat. Caution must be taken when reading these figures, as ideas and advice change often. It is also necessary to have sufficient vitamins, minerals and fluids.

Energy Systems

Food provides the fuel that is converted into energy. Carbohydrate is used first, then fat and finally protein. However, none of these stands alone and some fat will be used along with carbohydrate, along with a minimal amount of protein. However, apart from a tiny amount, protein is only used as a fuel when the other sources are depleted (see Chapter 5) – this is a big warning sign that over-exertion is taking place.

Carbohydrate, fat and protein are converted into glucose, fatty acids and amino acids, and these are used by the body to provide the necessary energy.

The glucose is stored in the muscles and liver as glycogen. The muscle glycogen is used as fuel (liver glycogen provides glucose to the brain). Although glycogen can be stored in the muscles and can increase with the effect of training, it is very

Food is abundant in most present-day societies.

Nutrition bars at the finish!

CARBOHYDRATES

Carbohydrate food can include:

- Complex carbohydrates:
  - cereals, grains and bread, porridge, pasta, rice, etc.
  - beans, kidney beans, baked beans, etc.
  - vegetables, fruit.
- Simple carbohydrates, e.g. sugar.

Most carbohydrate foods contain significant amounts of essential vitamins and minerals, and, in an unprocessed state, fibre.

Carbohydrates may be starches (complex carbohydrates) or sugars (simple carbohydrates). Generally, complex carbohydrates should be preferred, although when 'instant' energy is required, the simple carbohydrate comes into its own. Because the body's and muscles' carbohydrate stores are quickly used, athletes should ensure that they eat very soon after competition and training, within 20min is recommended, if possible. This will ensure that recovery is faster and that competition performance is improved. Even more importantly, drink a lot of water at all times.

Protein

Protein is essential for building and repairing body tissues. The continual stress that the body takes during intense training makes it essential that sufficient protein is taken in to repair and rebuild the body. However, as high-protein foods may also be high in fat, care should be taken. Vegetable-based protein contains lower fat than meat-based protein. High-protein foods can also take longer to digest and can cause discomfort if the runner is training more than once each day. Extra protein intake can't be stored in the body and is simply excreted.

Fat

Fat has the most concentrated source of food energy, with each gram of fat supply-

---

PROTEINS

Protein foods contain essential vitamins and minerals and may serve as a source of energy, if required.

- Animal protein: meat, fish and chicken; milk, cheeses, yoghurt, eggs.
- Plant protein: nuts and seeds.

---

ing nine calories (four for protein and carbohydrate). Good sources of fat are: butter, margarine, fatty meat, chicken skin, milk and cheese, ice cream, nuts and seeds.

Cholesterol and Saturated Fats

Cholesterol is present in meat, poultry and fish, milk and eggs. There is no cholesterol in fruit and vegetables, grains, nuts, seeds and dried beans and peas. High blood-cholesterol levels tend to increase the risk of heart disease, and saturated fats raise blood-cholesterol levels. Saturated fat is in the fats of whole milk, cream, cheese, eggs, butter, meat and poultry. Saturated fats solidify at room temperature.

Monounsaturated Fatty Acids and Polyunsaturated Fatty Acids

These types of fat may have a beneficial, lowering effect on blood-cholesterol levels. All fats, whether they contain mainly saturated fatty acids, monounsaturated fatty acids or polyunsaturated fatty acids, provide the same number of calories.

Fat can only be used as fuel aerobically (endurance-based exercise) whereas carbohydrate can be utilized both with and without oxygen.

Vitamins and Minerals

Although vitamin supplementation is not necessary for the majority of runners, they may be of benefit with very restricted diets of less than 1,200kcal/day, or with poor eating habits. In these cases, a low dose, broad-range nutritional supplement may help. Vitamins are necessary for red blood cell formation, for using oxygen and for metabolizing carbohydrate, protein

---

limited, and will become depleted during a long race or in hard training. Fat will then be used as the energy supplier but it is not a very efficient energy releaser and most people will train at a lower intensity when fat becomes the energy provider. Experienced athletes with a long history of endurance training are able to convert the fat more quickly and efficiently.

As fat is used more as a race progresses, the pace of most athletes will slow down when fat becomes the major energy provider. At the beginning of the marathon (and usually for all of the half-marathon) carbohydrate will be the major contributor, but later in the race a higher percentage of fat is used and its inefficiency will often be demonstrated by the athlete slowing down a lot, particularly with 'new' or inexperienced marathon runners.

Food Types and Sources

Carbohydrates

Carbohydrates provide the most energy and should form the basis of each meal.

and fat. With minerals, calcium is used in neuromuscular activity, and iron in oxygen transport. Iron deficiency can often occur amongst endurance runners (usually, but not always in female athletes). If iron is low, there is less available for haemoglobin formation (haemoglobin is the substance in the blood essential for carrying oxygen around the body) and its concentration decreases. The oxygen-carrying capacity of the blood depends on haemoglobin concentration and low levels are associated with a decrease in maximum oxygen uptake and therefore in physical working capacity. Iron-deficient (anaemic) individuals show symptoms of early fatigue, breathlessness and headaches. However, generally supplements are not necessary for runners eating a diet adequate in both quality and quantity.

Vitamins

Vitamins occur widely in many foods and are easily provided in a properly prepared, mixed diet containing fresh fruits and vegetables.

Unless an athlete is deficient in vitamins, vitamin supplementation is not required. Only the fat-soluble vitamins (A, D, E and K) can be stored (primarily in the liver), but a healthy runner eating a well-balanced diet will receive adequate amounts of all the essential vitamins. A vitamin deficiency may lower performance. A lack of the B vitamins normally has the most immediate effects, as does a lack of thiamine, while the effects of vitamin A deficiency may not appear for months. Care must be taken in cooking and preparing food as this may

VITAMIN AND MINERAL SUMMARY TABLE

Vitamin	Source	Functions
Vitamin A	Liver, carrots, dark green vegetables, fish, liver oil, eggs, butter, margarine.	Vitamin A helps to fight infections. It prevents bacteria and viruses from entering the body by keeping the cell walls strong. It is good for the skin and necessary for vision in dim light.
Vitamin B Group, e.g. Thiamine (B1), Riboflavin (B2), Niacin, Folic Acid (B12)	Milk, meat, fish, fruit, vegetables, cereals, eggs, nuts and bread.	Helps the breakdown of carbohydrate, protein and fat to release energy. Essential for the functioning of our nerves. The body cannot store the B vitamins for long, so a daily supply is important.
Vitamin C	Fresh and frozen fruit and vegetables. Products fortified with vitamin C.	Vitamin C is needed to fight infections, to help absorb iron from food and for healthy skin. A daily supply is necessary because it cannot be stored by our bodies.
Vitamin D	Produced by the body. Also in liver, fish oil, eggs, fortified breakfast cereals, butter and margarine.	Vitamin D is formed mainly by the action of sunlight on the skin. It helps the body to absorb and use calcium and phosphorus for strong bones and healthy teeth.
Vitamin E	Many foods, especially vegetable oils, eggs, green leafy vegetables.	Vitamin E helps to protect the cells.
Vitamin K	Produced by the body. Also green leafy vegetables, liver.	Vitamin K plays a vital role in the blood-clotting mechanisms.
Mineral	Source	Functions
Calcium	Milk, cheese, fish, beans, dark green vegetables.	Calcium forms the structure of bones and teeth. Because it is in constant demand, a regular supply is vital.
Iron	Meat, liver, dark green vegetables, peas, beans.	Iron is needed for the formation of red blood cells, which help to transport the necessary oxygen round the body.
Phosphorus	Liver, fish, poultry, eggs, cheese, milk, whole-grain, cereals, nuts.	Helps build bones and teeth and to regulate many internal activities of the body.

reduce the vitamin content (particularly vitamin C). Leaving the skin on fruit and vegetables, and steaming or micro-waving is better than frying.

Minerals

Minerals provide the substance for bones and teeth and are present in soft tissues and fluids, allowing the cells to work properly. Mineral supplementation will not help performance unless there is a deficiency. A poor diet may lead to deficiencies in iron and zinc.

Calcium

Very low calcium levels contribute to osteoporosis. In women, osteoporosis is generally caused by a drop in the level of the blood chemical oestrogen due to menopause or amenorrhea (lack of, few, or irregular periods), a low intake of calcium and a sedentary lifestyle.

Salt

Salt is needed by the body, but many people take too much and this can lead to high blood pressure. Salt is lost from the body through sweating but the kidneys increase their retention of salt (sodium)

and other electrolytes during exercise, so salt loss is low. Adding salt to food is only necessary with intense daily endurance training plus a hot environment plus a low sodium diet.

Zinc, selenium, sodium, potassium, iodine, chlorine, copper, manganese and magnesium are needed in tiny amounts and perform a variety of functions. They are found in a wide range of foods and deficiency is very rare.

Water and Fluids

Drinking adequately is essential for endurance runners during training and competition. The sweating and perspiration during exercise means that huge amounts of fluid are lost. If this fluid is not replaced, then dehydration occurs, stressing the body and leading to a decrease in performance and overheating. Water is the most suitable fluid to drink. Serious distance runners in training should drink 5ltr every day. Drinking is essential before, during and after training sessions. During training, runners may not realize that they are losing fluid and become dehydrated. Feeling thirsty is

not the sign that you should drink, drink often and lots. The colour of your urine is a good indicator of your hydration state; it will be a pale straw colour if you are well hydrated. A loss of as little as 2 per cent of body weight through fluid loss will have a significant effect on performance. Drinking in training will teach you to be comfortable about drinking when racing.

During marathon competition or long training sessions, it may be necessary to use carbohydrate drinks to supply energy to the muscles. It is important that the carbohydrate content of drinks is monitored carefully, as too much, although supplying energy to the muscles, will decrease the rate at which water can be assimilated. Water is the first priority and normally the carbohydrate content of drinks should be low.

There is little or no evidence that ergogenic aids improve performance, despite the various claims made for bee pollen, caffeine, carnitine, creatine and suchlike. However, despite this, caffeine is a stimulant and its psychological effects are to increase arousal, attention, motivation and concentration, and some endurance athletes have reported improvements in

ABOVE: Runners pass empty water bottles during the London Marathon.

RIGHT: A competitor tops up her water bottle during the London Marathon.

Competitors can leave their own drinks at water stations (left) or be content to drink the water supplied (above).

performance. On the downside, caffeine can be a diuretic causing extra fluid loss. It may also increase the resting metabolic rate, which may lead to extra heat production in the body.

Body Weight

One immediate factor when starting to train is the loss of weight (almost always body fat). Being either underweight or overweight can have an adverse effect on performance. Even in endurance events like marathon running, athletes may carry a higher ratio of muscle than non-athletes. Normal body weight charts should be treated with caution. If body fat loss is an aim, one way is to reduce the amount of fat taken in the diet. However, the best advice is to consult your doctor. Never go on a crash diet as these are likely to be missing in essential nutrients. This will undoubtedly affect performance, and indeed, your general health. If you want to lose weight, aim for a gradual weight reduction.

All distance runners in training will require more calories than people who don't run or exercise. However, it is important not to eat 'junk' food with high sugar and high calories. Complex carbohydrates include wholemeal bread, cereals, rice, potatoes, pasta, vegetables and fruit.

Checking Body Weight

Distance runners are extremely body-weight and body-fat conscious. There are various methods and formulae for assessing whether body weight/fat content is conducive to distance running. One method is described here but do be cautious if using this formula, it is a guide only and may not apply to all runners.

1   For men, start at 110lb for 5ft in height and add 5½lb for each inch above 5ft. So a 5ft 10in man should be 165lb (110 + 10 × 5½).
    For women, start at 100lb for 5ft in height and add 5lb for each inch above 5ft. So a 5ft 6in woman would be 130lb (100 + 6 × 5).
    These weights are the average for men and women.
2   For middle-distance and club-marathon runners, drop 10 per cent of this, so a male club-marathoner might weigh 149lb (165 − 16) and a female marathon runner 117lb (130 − 13)
3   For top-level and international marathon runners, rather than dropping 10 per cent, drop 15 per cent. So, an international male marathon runner might weigh as little as 140lb (165 − 25) and a female international marathon runner as little as 110lb (130 − 20).

'GOOD' TRAINING FOOD

Examples include: wholegrain cereal (e.g. muesli, Shredded Wheat, puffed wheat, Weetabix, bran flakes, porridge) with low fat milk and fruit, fruit juice, wholemeal sandwiches with tuna, chicken, lean meat, cottage cheese, egg, peanut butter, cheddar cheese, marmite, banana or salad items, baked potatoes and salad, baked beans and spaghetti.

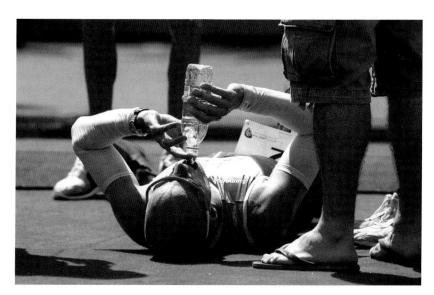

Please treat these figures with caution – they do not apply to runners under the age of 18 years old, or very small or very tall runners.

Eating for Racing

For professional and top-class runners, diet for training and racing is a part of their profession. However, for most of us, running is a part of life. It would be inadvisable to change your normal diet just days or the evening before a race. Don't think that you must start eating pasta if you hate it, just because some other people do. Stick with what you know. Generally, avoid fatty foods and too much protein, avoid food that will upset your stomach (including high-fibre food), and avoid too much sugary food or drink. Whatever you do, do have adequate water.

ABOVE: *Rehydration immediately after the finish is essential.*

BELOW: *Drinking straight after the finish at the World Marathon Championship.*

RIGHT: Food, drink and warmth at the end of the Athens Marathon.

Be careful not to eat too close to the race. Conversely, make sure that you do eat close enough so that you won't be hungry during the race, which would lead to a falling off in performance.

During very long races, your body craves solid food. Bananas, figs and energy bars are recommended for easy digestion and for not upsetting the stomach. Always try eating and drinking in training before doing so in races. Drink early and continue to drink throughout the race to maintain hydration throughout the race.

Immediately after the race, drink lots and make sure that you eat some carbohydrate food within twenty minutes, if possible. This will aid recovery from the race and will help to get you back to training quickly.

BELOW: Warmth and a hot drink when it's cold!

BELOW RIGHT: Cooking when camping before an event.

CHAPTER 11

WEIGHTS, RESISTANCE AND CORE WORK

Training for long-distance running can be very time-consuming, and athletes are always looking for short-cut gains and to save time. One of the ways that we might consider this is by careful use of weight and resistance training. However, any form of weight or resistance training should be geared specifically towards distance running.

Weight training is one of the most effective methods of developing muscular strength and local endurance. It is important to remember that marathon and half-marathon running is, above all, an endurance sport and that some consequences of weight training may not be beneficial to that. Any extra body-weight gained by lifting weights has to be carried along on that 13- or 26-mile journey, and carrying extra weight will be a disadvantage. To make the most use of weight training, you should be looking in three main areas:

1   Remedial work – if you are weak in one or more areas.
2   Strength – if you are weak, you won't get the best out of yourself.
3   Specific strength endurance – if there is a single muscle, or muscle group that is letting you down, then do something about it.

This chapter provides the basics to enable the runner to design and develop a basic schedule that will cater for individual needs. Weight training can be dangerous if done wrongly; it is best to receive proper instruction than to lift incorrectly.

We may not need the power and strength required by sprinters, but weight training can help distance runners.

What Main Muscle Groups Does the Distance Runner Need?

The major muscle groups are:

- Quadriceps, hamstrings and gastrocnemius/soleus (upper and lower legs).
- Hip flexors (abdominals-front legs attachments).
- Gluteals (backside/rear pelvis).
- Rectus abdominus and obliquus externus (stomach/abdominals).

However, despite running being (very obviously!) a leg and lower body activity, there is a need for some upper body strength as well. An efficient technique will require a 'balancing act' from the upper body and arms, and distance runners with a weak upper body should also look to do some remedial work in these areas as well.

Using resistance machines, as well as free weights, requires a little less skill and technique and the danger of injury – although present – is less.

A number of exercises are presented, most of which can be employed in using

---

EXERCISES FOR THE RUNNING MUSCLE GROUPS

Free Weights

- Deadlift – quads, gluteals.
- Clean – quads, gluteals, gastrocnemius (calves).
- Squat – quads, gluteals.

Resistance Lifts

- Leg curl – hamstrings, gastrocnemius.
- Leg press – quads, gluteals.
- Leg extension – quads.

Upper Body

The distance runner may well consider s/he doesn't need upper body or arm exercises; however, the bicep curl and tricep extension should be considered:

- Triceps extension – triceps.
- Bicep curl – biceps.

---

either free or resistance-type weight training. Always take advice and instruction from the experts. The deadlift, clean and the squat, particularly, should be treated with caution and only done under supervision.

Also, strong stomach and particularly core muscles are essential for the distance runner. There are a whole range of abdominal exercises. What is important is that the stomach muscles themselves are exercised. Generally, this will entail that the feet and legs are not held 'fixed', which will not isolate those muscles; they should be held free – many athletes working the stomach muscles properly in this way for the first time are amazed at the difference and at how much more difficult previously simple exercises become.

How Often?

Weight training is an extra to distance-running training. However, there is little point in starting to weight train unless there are going to be gains. I would suggest that twice a week would be the minimum, preferably three times per week. Many runners weight train through the off season and make great strength gains. As soon as the season begins, they stop weight training and are amazed when their new found strength starts to slip away! If you need to weight train, it may well be that you need to at least undergo a maintenance programme of weight training in the competition season

Warm-Up

It is necessary to be warmed-up properly. The usual strictures and recommendations apply (see Chapter 12).

How Heavy?

Before you start on a weights programme, you have to find out how much you are capable of lifting on each exercise. Test yourself to see how much you can lift on a single repetition. This is your maximum.

What Types of Schedule?

The number of repetitions and sets of exercises will be governed by the muscle group and the body area. Smaller muscles and muscle groups will tend to fatigue more quickly than large groups and should therefore be exercised later in the session

Weights Programme

Set out here is an example of a weight-training schedule for running. As an example, from the first group, for the first sets (quads and hamstring curl) 10 repetitions of quads are followed by 10 repetitions of hamstring curl, then 10 quads and so on.

Large muscle groups are exercised before small groups, and no group of muscles tired from exercise is immediately worked again.

The number of sets and repetitions are only guidelines, but have seemed in the past to have had maximum benefit without risking injury over overtiredness.

WEIGHT-TRAINING SCHEDULE

1 Quads (leg extensions): 3 × 10 × three-quarters maximum.
   Hamstring curl: 3 × 10 × two-thirds maximum.
   Work up to 3 × 15 repetitions, then increase weight.
2 Quads (half-squat): 3 × 10 × three-quarters maximum.
   Calf raise: 3 × 10 × three-quarters maximum.
   Work up to 3 × 15 repetitions, then increase weight.
3 Abdominals: push throughs to exhaustion. Repeat 3 times.
   Knee raise and straight leg shoot: to exhaustion.
   Fall back (eccentric movement): to exhaustion.

Then repeat 3 times.

The rest period between exercises and sets is kept to a minimum. However, care should be taken that you do not become so fatigued by adhering to a short recovery that good form is sacrificed when performing the exercise and the likelihood of injury is increased

All the weight-training exercises set out here are relevant to specific or general needs for distance runners. However, not all exercises will be appropriate for everybody. Only the specific exercises that are essentially required are fully explained.

Note: No pictures or diagrams are given. It is essential that correct instruction is given for weight training and it is possible that diagrams may be misleading. Ask for help from a qualified instructor.

Deadlift

Prime movers: quadriceps, gluteals, erector spinae.

- Place the toes underneath the bar with your feet about hip distance apart. Your feet may be pointing forwards or slightly outwards but they must be equidistant from both ends of the bar.
- Flex at the knees and hips to adopt the get set position with your arms positioned outside your knees and straight. Grasp the bar with an overhand grip. Ensure that your knees are correctly aligned with your feet and that your back is flat. your backside should be higher than your knees with your head looking forwards and slightly down.
- Position your shoulders slightly in advance of the bar to allow for a vertical line of travel of the bar upwards. Stand up, leading with your shoulders and keeping the bar close to your body throughout the movement,
- Ensure that your body moves to a full upright position without any hyper-extension at the knee joint.
- To return the bar – flex at the knees and hips and keep your back straight.

The Clean

Prime movers: quadriceps, gluteals, gastrocnemius, deltoids, trapezius, erector spinae, soleus, biceps.

This is an extremely complex lift. It is not appropriate to give an exhaustive list of coaching points or dictate a set teaching sequence as there are many ways of teaching the clean. The following is a general breakdown of the elements of the lift.

- The set: Flex at hips and knees with back straight. Look forward and slightly down. Keep knees over toes. Maintain feet at hip width apart, with shoulders in front of toes.
- Upright row onto toes phase: Ensure that weight is distributed over feet to maintain toe, ankle, knee alignment. Ensure that elbows are high at the end of the high pull phase.
- The receive phase: Come down on to heels and flex at the knees, and simultaneously bring elbows forward in advance of the bar, so the bar rests securely on the shoulders. Then stand up. To return, again keeping bar still, bring elbows high and above the bar. Lower under control to the thighs keeping bar close to the body. To return, reverse the deadlift.

Half Squat

Prime movers: quadriceps, gluteals.

- Clean the bar to the receive position. Bend your knees slightly and then extend them as the bar is pressed over your head to rest evenly on the top of your shoulders. Widen the grip to a comfortable distance but check that your hands are equidistant from both ends of the bar.
- Feet should be placed about hip width apart, either facing forwards or slightly outwards. In this starting position, your trunk should be upright and knees slightly bent.
- Squat down by bending at the knees and hips and ensure that your back is flat. Lower the bar in a vertical

line. Keep your head facing forwards throughout this movement and ensure that your knees travel in line with the feet.
- Squat to a position where thighs are roughly parallel to the ground – do not go beyond this level. Extend at your knees and hips to regain the upright position, ensuring that no hyper-extension occurs at your knee.
- To return the bar – narrow the grip, bend at knees slightly and then press the bar back over your head to the receive position. Return the bar to the floor as for the 'clean'.

Dumb-Bell Lunge

Note: Extra caution with this exercise.

Prime movers: quadriceps, gluteals.

- Deadlift the dumb-bells from the floor.
- Stand with feet hip width apart and toes facing directly forward. Step directly forward with right leg a sufficient distance to enable both knees to bend to a right angle as you lower your body.
- Keep body upright with toes forward. Keep feet hip width apart for stability. Look forward and slightly down. Ensure that trailing knee does not contact the floor. Relax shoulders and arms. Avoid excessive tension when gripping dumb-bells.
- Drive back with right leg to start position. Repeat alternating 'leading' legs.
- Reverse the deadlift to lower dumb-bells to the floor.

Exercises on Fixed-Resistance Machines

Leg Curl

Prime movers: hamstrings, gastrocnemius.

- Lie face down on the leg-curl machine with knees just over the edge of the bench and the ankles underneath the bottom pad. Hold on to the handles or the side of the bench. Curl the weight up by flexing your knees and keep your feet dorsi-flexed. Try to avoid any excess hip flexion (a certain amount is a natural function of the exercise).

- On no account hold your hips down on to the bench.
- Curl the bar through the full range under control, bringing the pad as close to your backside as possible. Lower slowly back to the starting position. Avoid letting the weight touch the weight stack. Repeat for the desired number of repetitions, breathing out as the weight is curled upwards. Make the action smooth and continuous.

Leg Press

Prime movers: quadriceps, gluteals.

- Sit on the seat and place your feet evenly on the foot plate, ensuring that the whole of the foot is in contact with the plate. Ensure also that your back is flat against the seat pad. Check that the knee angle is not less than 90 degrees.
- Grip the handles firmly at the side of the chair. Extend your legs under control until they are straight but without allowing your knees to hyper-extend.
- Return to the starting position working through the full range but without allowing the weight to touch the weight stack. Ensure that knees travel over the line of your feet throughout the movement.

Leg Extension

Prime movers: quadriceps.

- Sit on the leg extension machine and place your feet in a dorsi-flexed position beneath the lower pads.

- Sit well back on the bench so that the back of the knee joint touches the edge of the bench. Sit with your torso upright or leaning slightly backwards. Hold on to the handles or the edge of the bench (not too tightly) for support.
- Extend your legs under control until they are fully straight. Tilt the pelvis and take the lock off your knees.
- Narrow the grip to two thumb-lengths apart.
- Keeping the bar close to the body and leading with the elbows, raise the bar under control to just below chin level.
- Lower the bar under control to the starting position, avoiding rounding off the back, or hyper-extending the elbows.

Core-Conditioning Exercises

To run well it is essential to have good core muscles, those that sit beneath the abdominals, as well as strong abdominals.

Basic Balances: Organization and Time to Hold Positions

These basic balances are an enormous aid to core stability. I would suggest that the positions are held for 10sec to start with,

gradually working up by 5sec increments to a maximum of 30sec. Once this has been established, then a series of abdominal exercises should be added between each balance position. My suggestion would be to start with 10 repetitions and work up to the number of repetitions to fill 30sec. Some runners work up to as long as 90sec on the abdominal exercises but will all have started with 10 repetitions and worked up gradually.

1. Starting Position

Classic press-up position with both arms and legs supporting the body.

Aim for a straight line along the long axis from head through hips into legs, and maintain equal distance from the floor across the short axis, hip to hip, shoulder to shoulder … basically, don't drop your hips!

Arms should be held shoulder-width apart. Feet also apart, about the same distance as your arms. Feet should be balanced on toes, with toes pushing downwards directly below heels and not with heels either facing inwards or outwards.

As with all basic starting positions, allowances can be made for distance runners who do not have enough basic body strength (or perhaps, in this instance, balance) to begin. Specifically here, balance can be taken on the elbows rather than the hands, and knees rather than feet, if necessary. However, I would suggest that if it's necessary to do the basic starting position on both knees and elbows, then it might be better to pursue some remedial

Classic press-up position, both arms and legs supporting the body.

Plank position on elbows.

Plank position on elbows and knees.

One leg lifted.

One arm lifted.

balances before starting these basic core stability positions.

Positions 2–5
The next four positions consist of lifting and raising individually and in turn, each leg and each arm. Importantly, the stable position of a straight line along the long axis from head through hips into legs and *not dropping the hips* are the essential components of all these balance positions.

2. Left Leg Lift
Your foot and leg should be lifted with the foot at or just below hip level. The natural reaction of the body to this movement is to lift the left hip – this is where the real conditioning of core stability kicks in. The hips should *not* be raised or dropped but maintained in a level plane. Do use a mirror or friend or coach to ensure that your hips remain level.

3. Right Leg Lift
Exactly as before with the left leg, although of course the natural reaction will be to lift the right hip.

4. Left Arm Lift
Lift your arm so that it is parallel to the floor and pointing directly ahead. The natural reaction of the body to this movement is to lift the left hip and the left shoulder. Most runners find that is more difficult to maintain the essential 'flat' position when raising the arms rather than with the legs. Again, do use a mirror to ensure that your hips remain level.

5. Right Arm Lift
Exactly as before with the left arm. The reaction will be to lift the right hip and the right shoulder.

Positions 6 and 7: Opposite and Equal
These two positions consist of lifting and raising first, the left leg with the right arm, and, second, the right leg with the left arm.

6. Lift and Raise Left Leg with Right Arm
The usual response and reaction to this is to feel completely unstable. The hips will move up and down to react to the feeling

Opposite arm and leg lifted.

of instability; this is completely natural and is, of course, where the need for core stability comes in. Do persevere with this and the next balance (right leg, left arm) as they are the first of the more difficult ones and give tremendous improvements in core stability.

7. Lift and Raise Right Leg with Left Arm

As above, a feeling initially of great instability.

Positions 8 and 9: Star Balances

Balance is moved away from the basic starting position and taken to, first, the outside of the right foot, coupled with the right hand, and then the outside of the left foot,

Star position.

coupled with left hand. There should be a straight line through the right arm, chest and left arm at 90 degrees to the floor.

8. Star Balance on Right Leg and Right Arm

Start by lying on the floor on your right hip and right leg, with your right arm poised on the right hand. Lift your right hip off of the floor so that a straight line is made along the long axis of the body. The natural inclination is for the hips to fall back. It is essential to push the hips forward to hold the straight line and ensure core stability. Lift your left leg (this may not be possible when you start to use this exercise) and your left arm so that the left hand points directly upwards (straight line running through right arm, chest and left arm).

9. Star Balance on Left Leg and Left Arm

As above, but of course starting by lying on the floor on your left hip and left leg, with your left arm poised on the left hand.

Positions 10 and 11, Same Side Balances

These are very difficult balances. The two positions consist of lifting and raising, first, the left leg with the left arm, and, second, the right leg with the right arm.

10. Lift and Raise Left Leg with Left Arm

The usual response and reaction to this is to feel – once again – completely unstable. The right hip will lift considerably, as will the right shoulder. Your job is to gradually move your hip and shoulder downwards, with the eventual aim of establishing that straight line along the long axis from head through hips into legs, and a parallel line between hips and floor; don't drop your hips.

11. Lift and Raise Right Leg with Right Arm

As above, feeling of complete instability. Try to gradually force the left hip and shoulder back into straight line, parallel position.

Alternative Starting Position

The initial starting position is taken by balancing on your elbows rather than your hands. Essentially, the straight line position is maintained. The progressions ensue here by moving the elbows forward by a couple of inches on each succeeding balance. It is sometimes called a 'bridge' position.

RESISTANCE RUNNING

Hill running, running in sand, water running, running with a partner holding you back on stretch cords (caution), running with an object tied behind you (large car tyres are often quoted as an example; once again, caution) are all good training methods for gaining strength.

CHAPTER 12

STRETCHING AND FLEXIBILITY

Stretching along with a proper warm-up is often the last thing that we think about as runners, often citing that we don't have enough time. However, if we don't stretch, we will have plenty of time while we recover from injury. We stretch to develop flexibility and suppleness, and to improve the efficiency of the muscles to lengthen and to handle eccentric contraction (lengthening under resistance). Stretching trains the muscles to relax. **Flexibility** may be defined as the range of movement in joints, and stretching increases the range of movement in joints. **Suppleness** may be defined as the lengthening ability of the muscles, which will contribute towards increased flexibility in the joints.

Muscles that cause movement can also restrict movement because of negative tension. Our muscles are in a state of contraction for most of the time. They work by contracting. They may often be required to work repeatedly within their inner range and thus become shortened (they lose their ability to lengthen fully). This will have an adverse effect on eccentric contraction.

- By stretching muscles we allow them to relax to their full length, so that the full range of the muscle is employed, instead of remaining in a semi-contracted, tight, mid-range state.

Physical benefits are that we will be able to move better, feel physically more relaxed and be more able to cope with physical tasks. Getting the muscles to relax can have psychological benefits too, possibly by easing state of mind, increasing confidence and the ability to cope with mental tasks.

Muscles have elastic properties in that they have the ability to alter their length and return. They are not like rubber elastic, which stretches out and then relaxes back to its original shortened state. Muscles are contractile; they are relaxed at length and work by contracting.

Stretching is opening the muscle out to its full length and a bit further. This does create a tension in the muscle for a few moments, but a different tension than

when it contracts. Muscles spend a lot of time in a contracted state and need to be opened out and stretched regularly.

Stretching should always be carried out before a training session or race. It is important to include stretching after the muscles are well warmed-up.

If muscle fibres are going to tear, they will usually tear on sudden lengthening, or powerful eccentric contraction. With a forceful, explosive movement, the antagonist muscle, which is lengthening to control the movement, may not be able to cope with the speed and force of contraction, and fibres may be torn. Regular stretching of muscles enables them to cope more efficiently with this quick and powerful lengthening, which can occur in training and competition events.

WHY STRETCH?

Stretching serves to:

- relax muscle
- increase flexibility
- improve running performance
- reduce injury risk.

Sometimes it's necessary to stretch during the race.

Types of Stretching

Basically there are two types of stretching:

- Ballistic stretching:
  - Mobilizing exercises, which consist of gentle joint movements to stimulate the secretion of synovial fluid and to warm the muscles affecting that joint.
  - Ballistic bounces, where a muscle is opened to its full length and then is stretched by bouncing movements. (This method of stretching is not recommended as it can cause damage to the connective tissue in the muscle, may invoke a stretch reflex and may cause damage to muscle fibres).
- Static stretching: During static stretching we open the muscle to its full length and gently stretch it a little further, holding the position for a length of time. Static stretching can be further subdivided into:
  - Active stretching, when the performer carries out the stretch and holds the position.
  - Passive stretching, when the limb is moved and the stretch position is held by another person. (Passive stretching can also include exercises where gravity or any outside force causes a muscle to be stretched, rather than the concentric contraction of an opposing muscle).

With passive stretching we can carry out proprioceptive neuromuscular facilitation (PNF) stretching, sometimes referred to as contract–relax stretching because having held a muscle in a stretch position for a length of time, we can then get the muscle to contract forcefully and isometrically against a strong resistance for a few seconds and then get it to relax and lengthen further. This phenomenon occurs because we invoke an inverse stretch reflex (a neurological response) in the muscle, which causes the muscle fibres to relax in response to high tension.

PNF stretching is perhaps better carried out passively with the assistance of another person, although it can be performed actively. Either way, the muscle to be stretched is moved slowly into its maximum (yet comfortable) lengthened position and is held there for a number of seconds. Then the muscle is contracted isometrically for about 5sec against a resistance from the partner.

Stretch Reflex

Within muscles are proprioceptors in the form of muscle spindles, which resemble a coiled wire around muscle fibres. When a muscle is stretched (even the smallest lengthening), the stretch is sensed by the spindle and a message is sent via a sensory nerve to the central nervous system (CNS). A message returns via a motor nerve to the muscle fibre telling it to contract. Stretch reflex is, therefore, the basis of muscle tone.

Inverse Stretch Reflex

If a muscle is subjected to excessive tension, as might happen when suddenly subjected to a very heavy resistance, the excessive tension is sensed by other proprioceptors, this time in the muscle–tendon junction. These sensory organs are known as Golgi tendon organs (GTO). When the GTO senses excessive stretch, a message is sent to the CNS and a message returns telling the muscle fibres to relax. In this way it acts as a safety device, protecting the muscle fibres from forces that could otherwise damage them.

Stretching for Development or Maintenance

The bulk of the muscle consists of bundles of muscle fibres bound together by an inelastic connective tissue made of collagen. We can stretch muscles to develop flexibility or to maintain existing flexibility. When we stretch muscles, we are attempting to maintain or increase the lengthening ability of the muscle. In order to increase the ability of the muscle to lengthen, we need to stretch the connective tissue within the muscle and increase the elongation potential of the muscle fibres.

Ballistic stretching does not increase the length of the connective collagen tissue, though it does have an effect on the muscle fibres. By bouncing a muscle, therefore, we can actually cause damage to the collagen fibres, which can result in muscle pain and not necessarily any increase in the relaxation potential of the belly of the muscle.

Although the collagen fibre is comparatively inelastic, when warm it can become more pliable and can be permanently elongated. If cold, it is brittle and can be damaged, and this is the reason why stretching exercises should always be carried out in warm conditions and when the muscle is well warmed-up. If stretches are being carried out as part of the preparatory warm-up before training or sport, they will occur after the mobilizing and elevation of heart rate components of the warm-up.

Maintenance stretches might be those stretches carried out as part of the warm-up before activity, or as part of the cool-down at the end of any activity. This type of stretching will involve slowly opening the muscle to its full length, stretching it gently a bit further so that an amount of comfortable tension is developed and holding the stretch position for between 7 to 10sec. If stretching is for the development of flexibility, we need to hold the stretch much longer; about 20 to 30sec.

This can be carried out in three progressive stages (the progressive stretch method):

1. Very slowly and gently ease the muscle into a comfortable lengthened position. This allows the muscle to become desensitized (it cancels out the stretch reflex) and becomes accustomed to the lengthened state. Hold this comfortable stretch for about 7sec.
2. Maintain the position but slightly increase the stretch tension very

slowly and gently and hold for another 7sec. This now allows the warm collagen connective tissue fibres to stretch (known as 'creeping').

3 Maintain the stretch position but now increase the stretch tension slightly more and hold for a further 7sec. This allows the muscle fibres to elongate along with the connective tissue.

In this way you will have held the stretch position for approximately 21sec. Not all muscles of the body require developmental stretching, but those major muscles prone to shortening do, otherwise full range of movement will be restricted affect.

Marathon and half-marathon running should involve a high percentage of leg power (although many runners do not do the strength training required for this) and will require the athlete to develop suppleness in quadriceps (front of the thigh), hamstrings (back of the thigh), calf muscles (gastrocnemius and soleus – back of the lower leg), anterior tibial muscles (front of the lower leg), gluteals (buttocks), adductors (inner thigh), and hip flexors (ilio-psoas – deep muscles attached to the lumbar spine and to the inside of the femur; they lift up the thigh, and the stretch tension will be felt in the groin/top thigh region).

All the above muscles should be stretched as part of the warm-up (after gentle, low-intensity activity to warm the muscles), and at the end of a training session or competition, as a vital part of the

cool-down, and thus become an important part of the training programme.

I would particularly recommend a fairly long stretching session, involving all the above mentioned, at the end of every training run.

Stretching Exercises

Lower Body and Legs: the Calf Muscles at the Back of the Lower Leg (Gastrocnemius, Soleus)

This free-standing calf stretch is a gentle stretch and is often performed as part of the pre-stretch and post-stretch components of a warm-up and warm-down to a training session.

Stand with one foot forward and one foot back, both feet pointing forwards (it is important that the back foot is pointing directly forwards). Bend the knee of the front leg and allow your body weight to come forward over that leg. Keep the back leg straight and the heel down to the floor. Hold that position for about 7 to

10sec and the stretch will occur in the calf region of the back leg, emphasizing the gastrocnemius muscle. Change over legs and repeat.

From the above position, bend the back leg slightly and bring your bodyweight backwards so that it is over the back leg (often the position is described as sitting on an imaginary bar stool). Keep the heel of the back foot down on the floor, hold for about 7 to 10sec, and the stretch is now emphasized in the soleus muscle of the calf. This free-standing exercise is often used as part of the pre-stretch and post-stretch components of a warm-up and warm-down to a training session.

Stand facing a wall with your feet together about 1m away from the wall. Lean towards the wall, supporting your body weight with outstretched arms. Lower your heels down to the floor (comfortable stretch emphasizing the gastrocnemius or outer calf muscles).

Stand facing a wall with both feet about 1m away from the wall. Place one foot forward closer to the wall. As with the previous exercise, lower the heel of the

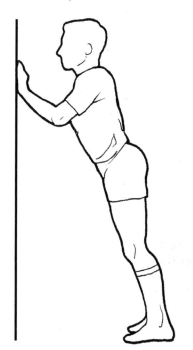

Progressive calves and Achilles tendon stretch.

Progressive calves and Achilles tendon stretch.

Progressive calves and Achilles tendon stretch.

rear foot towards the floor and hold for about 7 to 10sec, thus stretching the gastrocnemius muscle of that rear leg. As flexibility increases, you can move the rear foot further back to increase the stretch, as well as bending the arms to lower the body towards the wall.

Change over legs and repeat.

Stand facing a wall, but this time a little closer to the wall. Place one foot up to the wall with the foot dorsiflexed (toes up) against the wall and heel on the floor. Flex the knee of that leg so that it moves towards the wall and the stretch will be felt in the lower part of the calf muscles of that leg (i.e. soleus is emphasized). Hold for about 7 to 10sec. Change over legs and repeat.

Anterior Tibial Muscle at the Front of the Lower Leg

Kneel on the floor with toes pointing back, so that you are sitting on your heels. Allow your body weight to press downwards to exaggerate the plantar-flexion of the feet.

Bodyweight can be adjusted to reduce or increase the stretch tension. (Remember, keep within the limits of pain and adjust bodyweight by lifting slightly off the heels to start with).

The anterior tibial muscle can also be stretched while stretching the quadriceps muscles in a standing or prone (face-down) position, as will be evident in the next section.

Quadriceps Muscles at the Front of the Thigh

Lie face-down on the floor. Bend one knee and take hold of the foot of that leg with the hand and gently pull that foot towards the buttock. Press the hip down towards the floor. Hold the position for about 7 to 10sec.

It may be emphasized by some good exercise teachers that to reduce the strain on the metatarso-phalangeal joints (the toes with the bones of the foot), the foot should be held and not the toes. However, if the toes are held, then stretch is also achieved in the anterior tibial muscle at the same time. Advice about not holding the toes might be given to the non-athlete aiming for health-related fitness in an exercise class.

Stand either free and in balance, or holding on to a partner or wall. Flex one knee and lift the foot of that leg towards the buttock. Grasp that foot with the hand and gently pull the heel of that foot in towards the buttock, at the same time pushing the hip forwards (this pushing forward of the hip is important in order to achieve a full stretch of rectus femoris, which crosses the hip joint. Keep that thigh pointing downwards, close to, and in line with, the thigh of the supporting leg.

Hamstrings at the Back of the Thigh (Biceps Femoris, Semitendinosus, Semimembranosus)

Tight hamstrings can be particularly prone to injury. Therefore the development and maintenance of suppleness in this group of muscles, and the consequent flexibility of the knee and hip joints, are essential.

To effect proper relaxation in the hamstrings during stretching, and to ensure maximum safety for the lumbar spine, it is important that the correct technique is carried out, and some traditional methods of stretching the hamstrings are no longer recommended.

The hamstring muscles cross both the knee joint and the hip joint, and to fully stretch the muscles, the knee must be extended (straight) and the hip flexed (the thigh forwards). However, if a person is particularly inflexible because of tight muscles, the full extension of the knee joint in particular may not be possible at first and should not be forced.

Free-standing, one foot in front of the other, with the front leg straight and the back leg bent at the knee, feet facing forwards. Bend forward from the hip joint and support body weight on the arms by resting your hands on the thigh of the bent leg. The stretch should be felt in the back of the thigh of the front straight leg. Achieve a full stretch by lifting the hips and buttocks backwards and upwards.

Stand facing a low step, bench, chair or exercise bar (depending on present flexibility and the height required), which will act as a support. Lift one leg and rest it straight on the support. Keep the standing leg slightly 'soft' (knee very slightly bent). Slowly bend forward from the hip joint to achieve a very comfortable stretch and hold the position for about 7sec. Then slightly increase the stretch tension, but still within comfort, and hold for a further 7sec. Increase the stretch tension further, but well within the limits of pain, and hold for a further 7sec (the progressive stretch method). The stretch will be felt in the hamstrings of the leg resting on the support. Do not overstretch these muscles, otherwise contractile tension will develop – the opposite to what we want to achieve.

A safe and effective way of stretching the hamstrings is to sit with one leg straight and outstretched along a bench and the other leg bent, down by the side of the bench, with your foot resting on the floor. Bend forwards from the hip joint until a comfortable stretch can be felt in the hamstrings of the straight, supported

Hamstring stretch.

leg and hold for about 7 to 10sec for maintenance, or longer using the progressive stretch method for development

Another comparatively safe developmental stretch for the hamstrings (although I feel having substantial effect on the gluteals) can be achieved by lying face up with knees flexed and feet resting flat on the floor. Lift one leg and grasp the back of the thigh with your hands. Gently pull that leg towards your chest, as far as comfort will allow. Slowly move your hands down the leg and attempt to grasp the leg around the calf region, which will enable you to try to extend the knee joint.

Many people will find it difficult to extend (straighten) the knee at first, and with a flexed knee, full stretch of the hamstrings is not possible. However, this exercise is safe and effective for beginners concerned with health-related fitness.

Unsafe and Not Recommended

The traditional method of stretching the hamstrings by standing feet together (or even feet crossed-over), legs straight and bending forwards to reach towards the toes, should be absolutely discouraged as ineffective and potentially dangerous for the lower back.

If we were to adopt this position and bounce as well (ballistic stretch), it becomes an extremely dangerous exercise because of stretch reflex invoked in the hamstring muscles and the consequent possibility of muscle tears, and because of the severe pressure at the pivot point in the lumbar vertebrae with the possibility of intervertebral disc damage, nerve impingement and back muscle strain.

When we are in a standing position, both the quadriceps at the front of the thigh and the hamstrings at the back of the thigh are constantly contracting concentrically (shortening) and eccentrically (lengthening) to hold a standing posture against the force of gravity. Stretch reflex is therefore constantly occurring in both groups of muscles, which results in muscle-fibre contraction. If we bend forward the hamstring muscles are stretched, yet still attempt to contract in order to maintain posture. Therefore, we cannot achieve a relaxed lengthening in these muscles, but instead a degree of tension. For that reason it is an ineffective and inefficient method of stretching the hamstrings.

The danger of this position has already been dealt with to some degree. To bend forwards with straight legs (extended knees) can be very dangerous for the lower back.

Tremendous leverage is applied to the pivot point, which may be the lumbar spine in inflexible people. This results in considerable compression on the anterior (front) aspect of the intervertebral discs, with the possibility of disc prolapse or herniation at the back of the spine. Bulging discs can then impinge on nerve roots, which can result in leg pain and back pain.

Also, in this position, the extensor muscles of the spine cannot function properly and have little supporting effect, and the weight of the upper body is borne by the many tiny ligaments of the vertebral column. Muscles may go into spasm in an attempt to protect the spine, or may even tear in an attempt to eccentrically contract.

Adductor Muscles of the Inner Thigh

It is important to stretch the adductor muscles of the inner thigh as they assist the action of the quadriceps and hip flexors during running, especially when running up hill, and can be prone to strain and origin inflammation when tight.

Stand with legs fairly wide apart. Turn one foot slightly to the side and bend the knee of that leg so as to lunge to that side. Keep the body facing forwards and do not turn to the lunge side. Keep the other leg straight and the foot of that leg pointing forwards and flat on the floor. Hold for about 7 to 10sec. Feel the stretch on the inner thigh of the straight leg. Repeat with the other leg.

Important:

1   Do not lunge too far, which could place excessive stress on the knee joint. Keep the knee of the lunge leg

Stretching the adductor muscles.

Stretching the adductor muscles.

within the line of the toes of that foot.

2 Keep the foot of the straight leg pointing forwards and do not allow it to roll on to the medial (inner) aspect, which could place excessive stress on the joint of the big toe.

Sit on the floor with knees bent and the soles of your feet together, back straight. Rest your hands on the inner thighs, just above the knees. Use your arms to press downwards, which will further abduct the hip joints and thus stretch the adductor muscles of the inner thigh. Alternatively, you could take hold of your ankles and use your elbows to force the thighs apart.

Hold a comfortable stretch for about 7 to 10sec, or use the progressive stretch method for development.

Active PNF Stretch of the Adductors

You can also carry out your own PNF stretch in this position: press downwards with your arms for about 7sec, then relax the pressure and try to push your thighs together against the strong resistance of your arms. This produces a strong isometric contraction of the adductor muscles. Hold this contraction for about 4sec and then relax for 1 or 2sec. Repeat the stretch, pushing downwards on the thighs and hold for about 7sec again. You should experience a greater range of muscle lengthening on the second stretch. This is because the Golgi tendon organ in the adductor muscle tendon sensed a very strong contraction and brought about a relaxation in the muscle fibres.

Repeat the procedure a number of times, obtaining greater stretch each time. As it can be fairly tiring to carry out an active PNF stretch, it may be better to recruit the help of a responsible partner.

Abductor Muscles and the Outer Thigh (Gluteus Medius, Tensor Fascia Latae, Ilio-Tibial Band)

The stretching of this region can be very valuable for runners, who may otherwise suffer pain on the outer side of the knee due to inflammation of the ilio-tibial band caused by repetitive friction from tight tissue. Stretching of the abductor muscles can help reduce that tension in the connective tissue.

Sit on the floor with legs outstretched. Cross the right leg over the left leg with the right foot flat on the floor on the outer side of the left knee. Rest the right hand on the floor behind you with the arm straight to support your upper body. With your left hand, pull the right knee gently over to the left. Hold for about 7 to 10sec and feel the stretch in the top of the outer right hip region. Repeat with the other leg.

Gluteal Muscles of the Buttock (Gluteus Maximus – Hip-Extensor Muscle)

Lie on your back with your knees bent and feet flat on the floor. Keeping one foot on the floor and that knee bent, tuck the other leg up towards your chest and place your hands behind your thigh, linking fingers. Pull that thigh in towards the chest. Hold that stretch position for about 10 or 20sec and feel the stretch in that particular buttock. Repeat with the other leg.

Relax the upper body and keep your head resting back on the floor. Keep the other leg bent with the foot flat on the

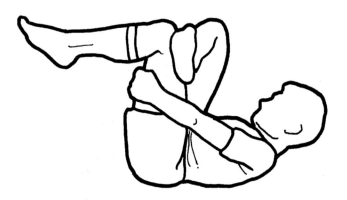

Stretching the glutes.

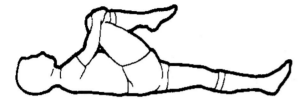

Hip flexor stretch.

floor. Do not lift the pelvis too high off the floor.

Lie on your back with knees bent and feet flat on the floor. Lift one leg and cross it over the other leg, which is still resting with the foot on the floor (rest the outside of the ankle of the raised leg on the knee of the lower leg). This will laterally rotate the raised leg slightly. Now lift the lower leg slightly and place your hands round the back of that thigh, linking fingers. Gently pull that thigh towards your chest and the stretch will occur in the gluteal at the top of the leg that is crossed. Hold for about 10 or 20sec. Repeat with the other leg.

Try to relax the upper body and keep the head resting back on the floor.

Hip-Flexor Muscles (Ilio-Psoas)

Iliacus and psoas major share a common insertion on the lesser trochanter on the medial aspect of the femur.

Achieve a wide lunge position with one leg forwards, foot flat on the floor (but be sure to have your knee over that foot and not beyond it), and the other leg well backwards with knee resting on the floor (with toes either pointed backwards or curled under). Push your hips forwards and downwards, while lifting the upper body slightly towards the vertical (but not straining to erect the spine).

You may wish to rest both your hands on the floor, or perform the exercise by the side of a bench so that you can hold on to the bench.

Mobilizing and Stretching Exercises for the Back

Muscles involved include erector spinae, obliques; also mobilizes spinal joints.

Lie on your back with knees tucked up towards your chest. Place your hands behind the thighs or around the shins. Link fingers and pull the knees further towards your chest, lifting the pelvis off the floor. Hold for between 7 to 10sec.

Lie on your back. Tuck your knees towards the chest and bring the legs over your head either to rest on a support (chair, bench or step) or to the floor behind your head. (Do not lift two straight legs up and over your head.) Hold for about 7sec and slowly and carefully return. Repeat as desired. If the back of your neck is particularly weak, or if there is any

Stretching the back.

cervical spinal damage, do not perform this exercise, as stress is placed on the neck.

Lie on your back with knees well bent, feet flat on the floor and fairly close to your buttocks. Place outstretched arms to the sides. Gently lower both knees down to the floor to one side, and then across to the other side. Repeat the movement as many times as desired.

Lie on your back with arms outstretched to the sides and legs straight. Tuck the left leg towards arms chest. With the right hand, take hold of the outer side of the left thigh close to the knee and pull over towards the floor on the right side of the body. Your body will twist and roll over to some degree, but try to keep the left arm and shoulder on the floor.

Psoas Position for the Relief of Lower Back Pain

A lot of the stiffness and pain experienced occasionally in the lower back is because of muscle spasm. The extensor muscles, in particular, protectively tighten up when the spine is put into a potentially danger-ous position, as might result from forward bending while load-bearing, incorrect lifting posture, and so on.

To help those tight muscles to relax, the psoas position passively shortens the hip flexor muscles and reduces the tension they normally apply to the lumbar spine.

Lie on the floor on your back with your legs up and over a firm support. If the support is fairly low, it will still have an effect, although it is perhaps better if the support is about the height of a chair or bed, so that your thighs are almost vertical and at 90 degrees to your trunk. Relax in this position for about 20min, and repeat two or three times per day for two or three days.

Passive Stretches and PNF Stretches with a Partner

When another person is acting as a partner to help you with passive stretching and PNF stretching, that person must act very carefully, responsibly and must be fully aware of, and sympathetic to, your limitations. Moves must be carried out smoothly and slowly, with constant communication between both of you. Care must be taken not to exert excessive pressure over joints.

Hamstrings

Lie back on the floor with knees bent and feet flat on the floor. Your partner kneels near your legs, takes hold of one leg (which is straightened) and with one hand on the front of your thigh and the other against the back of your heel, raises that leg, flexing the hip. If your partner also allows the heel of the foot of your straight leg to rest on his/her shoulder, then their body weight can be used by leaning forwards and pushing the straight leg up.

Both you and your partner should continually communicate verbally.

When your limit has been reached, hold the position for 7 to 10sec for maintenance, or 20 to 30sec for development. Repeat a number of times, and repeat with the other leg.

PNF Stretching of the Hamstring

Exactly the same procedure is carried out as described above, but this time the stretch position is held for about 7sec. Then you push back with your straight leg as hard as possible against the resistance of your partner for about 4sec. (This

causes a strong isometric contraction in the hamstrings and gluteals, which triggers the GTOs to relax the muscles.) Tension is released for a couple of seconds and then the stretch can be applied again for another 7sec. By the second stretch, a greater range should be achieved.

Adductors

Sit on the floor with legs bent and the soles of your feet together. You could either sit free with arms supporting you behind or you could rest your back against a wall.

Stretching to lengthen muscles.

Your partner kneels in front of you, places his/her hands on the inside of your knees and, with straight arms, allows body weight to press downwards, thus opening your thighs (abducting the hip joints).

PNF Stretch of the Adductor Muscles with a Partner

The same procedure is carried out as described above, but this time the stretch is held for about 7sec. Then you push back for about 4sec, trying to close your thighs, against the resistance of your partner. The tension is released for a couple of seconds and then the stretch is applied again for another 7sec.

By the second stretch, a greater range should be achieved.

FINAL NOTE

The importance of mobility and flexibility cannot be overemphasized. For many distance runners, it may be the key to a significant increase in performance.

Lisa Fawcett even manages to stretch after completing a marathon while talking to supporters.

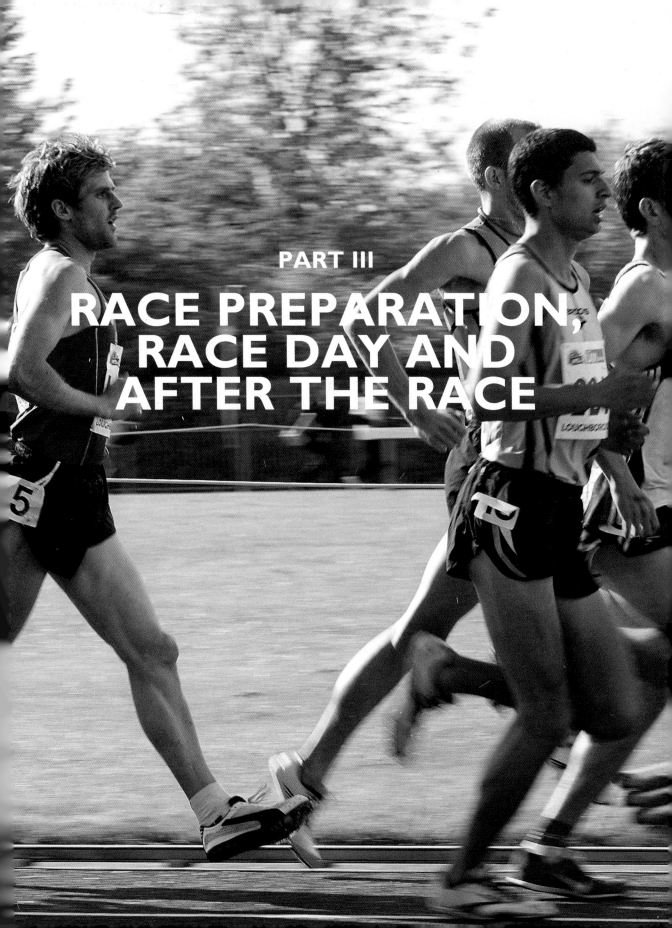

PART III

RACE PREPARATION, RACE DAY AND AFTER THE RACE

CHAPTER 13

TAPERING AND RACE PREPARATION

Preparation for competition begins with the first training session ever done. For competing runners, rather than 'keep-fit' people who use a little running to do just that, competition is the reason for all the training; finishing the marathon or half-marathon in a respectable time is what the training is for. However, there are some runners who do train hard and efficiently but are unable to compete as well as their training would indicate. It is important to examine why this is. Sometimes it can be nervousness approaching a race, perhaps a dislike of competition, sometimes it can be training too hard immediately prior to a race. This can be summed up as poor pre-race preparation.

Poor Pre-Race Preparation

This can be broken into a number of things including those factors above, but also: little knowledge of the course, inappropriate kit or equipment, a lack of proper food, lack of sleep, and arriving at the race venue too late. These factors occur immediately before the event. The factor that is often misunderstood, and can be misused because of that misunderstanding, is the preparation for the race called tapering.

Tapering can be difficult to explain and is perhaps the least understood of all the different aspects of training, but in short can be called the change of training in preparation for a race. This change is usually to less training. Training is physically challenging and fatiguing; approaching a race and maintaining hard training will mean going into the race tired and unlikely to maximize performance. Training hard leads to tiredness; training less leads to

Winning the World Marathon title requires careful planning and tapering.

recovery. This may sound simplistic and, of course, there are many factors to take into account. However, the major purpose of a taper phase is to allow athletes to recover from the fatigue of hard training before an important race. This requires maintaining the fitness level and minimizing the fatigue level.

All runners are often reluctant to reduce the amount of their training as the fear is that all the hard-won fitness and conditioning will be lost in the tapering period. This belief is untrue. Physiological changes and gains through hard training will be maintained even if training is reduced by 50 per cent. It is a so-called 'simmering' effect. Tapering ensures recovery from the hard training. Two things are critical:

1   The quantity, quality and types of training in the hard training period.
2   The quantity, quality and types of training in the taper period.

Without the hard training period, the taper period will have little effect.

During the taper period there will be an increase in glycogen levels because of the extra rest, a maintenance of blood volume levels, a maintenance or increase in muscle strength, and a maintenance in aerobic capacity. However, these will not just occur as if by chance. It is necessary to examine the type and amount of training during that taper period.

Types of Taper

Three types of taper have been widely used in many competitive sports:

*   The rest-only taper (ROT). This is self-explanatory. For a period of time before the race, the athlete stops training and rests only.
*   The low-intensity taper (LIT). Quality training ceases and training is maintained by low-intensity (easy) running.
*   The high-intensity taper (HIT). The amount of time spent training is reduced, while the intensity is maintained or increased. The general

Perfect preparation makes for perfect performance.

PROGRESSIVE HIT

Here is a simple example of progression in a HIT in distance running. It is assumed that the runner has trained hard and consistently using interval running, as well as pure endurance running.

*   7 days before the race, a steady run of between ⅓ and ½ of the race distance, i.e. for a marathon, between 9 and 13 miles; for a half-marathon, between ½ and ¾ of the race distance, say 7 to 10 miles.
*   6 days before the race, 6 × 1000m at best race-pace for 10,000m, with 60sec recovery-interval. For a half-marathon, perhaps 5 × 800m at best 5,000m or 10,000m pace, 60 to 90sec recovery-interval.
*   5 days before the race, 1h run with a few fast 30sec stride-outs, adequate steady running in between. For the half-marathon, perhaps 45min with the fast strides.
*   4 days before race, 5 × 800m at best 5,000m pace, 75sec rest-interval. For the half-marathon, 4 × 800m.
*   3 days before the race, for both marathon and half-marathon, 30min run with a few fast(er) 30sec stride-outs, adequate steady running in between.
*   2 days before race, rest or very easy, short run, but rest advised.
*   Day before the race (both distances), 12 to 15min run with some very short, fast bursts to stretch legs and 'wake up' fast twitch muscles; 2 × 100m in 60sec, 60sec rest-interval.

principles are: less training time, more intensity, more recovery.

In most cases, ROT and LIT do not work efficiently. LIT makes little or no difference to a race performance, although it is fair to say that many runners feel the 'need' to run even the evening before a race. If running will make you feel psychologically better, then a short, easy jog may be appropriate. However, ROT may even reduce race performance.

The best taper is HIT. The amount of training during the taper period is reduced in amount and time, but the intensity of the session is increased. The amount of recovery between the efforts will also be greater. It may be necessary to increase carbohydrate intake, although caution should be exercised because it is easy to increase body weight by eating the same amount while exercising and training less. Water intake should be increased. The amount of training should be reduced to between 66 per cent and 50 per cent (or even less). Tapering is crucial for best race performance but is only effective if combined with hard training before the race season.

Important Factors on Tapering

If training has not been hard and consistent, there is little point in undertaking a taper period. Training must be hard for a taper to be efficient. It is important to do something the day prior to a race. While it is important to be rested, too much rest will lead to lethargy, a feeling of tiredness. A very short training session, perhaps as little as 10 or 15min will ensure that the fast twitch muscles are prepared.

The same taper does not work for everybody. It is important to experiment before deciding if a taper works, and if so, which type of taper.

Apart from the physical and mental aspects of tapering and preparing for a race, there are other, less complicated issues to consider, such as food, accommodation, travel and clothing and equipment.

Racing over shorter distances helps on a taper.

Don't make changes to your usual food and diet before a race, there is no perfect pre-race food and changing normal habits may lead to an upset stomach. A good night's rest is ideal but not always possible. Always try to find suitable accommodation. Give yourself sufficient time to check the start and where to leave your warm clothes if the race finishes at a different place (viz. Virgin London marathon). Ensure that your race kit is suitable. Also remember to take safety pins, a water

bottle, toilet paper and Vaseline. Remember to have warm clothing for immediately after the event

Preparation Makes Perfect

Successful racing depends on attention to detail and early preparation. Leaving things late and to chance will almost guarantee

1 When the amount of training is reduced, there are a lot more hours to fill, particularly before a race. It is easy to sit around with other runners and drink and eat more than normal. If you have eaten and prepared properly, then extra, possibly junk, food will not help you race better.

2 Although many people think that you do not need to taper for unimportant races, do remember that a marathon particularly is extremely physically tiring at whatever speed you run and you do need to be rested before the event.

3 The individual athlete's reaction to pre-race nerves and anxiety will also determine the exact kind of taper.

4 Mental preparation is at least as important as physical tapering, do not ignore this aspect.

5 Tapering too often loses its efficiency. Early season and shorter, unimportant races should be 'raced through' without too drastic a taper.

6 Older runners may require a longer taper than younger runners.

7 Too much tapering may lead to a loss of conditioning. Do not taper too often or too much.

failure. Check your shoes and clothing one week before. Ensure that your travel and accommodation is booked and correct. Maps and emergency contact telephone numbers must be close to hand.

On the day before the race, recheck your shoes and clothing, have a water bottle and energy snack ready all the time. Carry the race details with you. Go to the race briefing, if there is one. If there isn't, there will almost certainly be a help-desk close to the race registration. Don't be afraid to ask questions, but do make sure that the questions aren't already answered in the race literature. Importantly, ensure that you know your start time. Check event course and routes; drive around the course, if it's open to traffic.

Eat sensibly, don't overeat and stay with food that you are comfortable with. If you are unsure about nearby restaurants, take your own food with you. Try to sleep, but if you suffer from pre-race nerves then don't worry, just rest. Be aware that most athletes have disrupted sleep the night before an event. Check water bottles and all race numbers. Ensure that they are attached where they should be.

Immediate Pre-Race Preparation

In Great Britain, morning starts are the norm, particularly for marathons. It is important to have adequate time before the event, so timetable in extra time in case there are any delays in your schedule. Be prepared for traffic conditions to slow you down and have an idea of where you will

park at the race venue. It is important to eat breakfast, however nervous you feel. Drink adequately. Water is to be preferred but there is nothing wrong with tea or coffee. Do timetable in more than one toilet visit and ensure that you know where they are located at the race venue.

Give yourself adequate time to prepare yourself at the start area. Mentally prepare for the event; visualize what you will do and then check your starting line and, if appropriate, where your anticipated finishing time will start. At the Virgin London Marathon, these are indicated every 10min, e.g. 2h 10min, 2h 20min, etc. down to 4 h and even easier pacings. *Do not promote yourself to a faster start/finish time*, you will go out too fast and pay the price later in the race.

Stretching and warming up are an individual choice; start areas can be very busy and noisy before the beginning of a race. If you need to be calm and quiet before a race, ensure that you have found a suitable place to mentally prepare. Finally, breathe slowly and visualize yourself doing well; tell yourself that if anything goes wrong, you will deal with it immediately and not let it spoil your race. Focus on the first few miles.

Post-Race

Eat and drink as soon as possible, it will help recovery. Dress in warm clothes. If possible, stretch and have a massage.

CHAPTER 14

PRECAUTIONS FOR OLDER RUNNERS AND FOR FEMALE RUNNERS

Age

Sadly, there is no antidote for getting older, not even hard exercise or training. However, there is some evidence that people who are very active throughout their lives may offset the ageing process. The majority of the (sedentary) population will lose approximately 8 to 10 per cent of their VO_2max every ten years after their mid-twenties, along with a lessening of muscle contractibility and muscle mass. However, in active runners this loss can be halved.

Be Realistic in Training

Running while getting older does mean that training has to be realistic. Running training is physically stressful on the body and to attempt to keep training and running at the same intensity and speed will lead to injury, disillusionment and quite possibly a dislike of running. As we get older, more recovery time is needed, particularly if training is a mixture of endurance, speed, interval and repetition running, rather than the introductory training of slow and long. This certainly doesn't mean that good performances will stop; there are runners (men) in their forties

and fifties still capable of running 2.15 and 2.20 for the marathon, respectively. This will not apply to the majority of us but is a reflection of how world-class performers from their younger years can maintain speed and endurance despite getting older. Taking a day off between hard sessions, or perhaps substituting cycling or swimming on the 'in-between' days, is advisable. Certainly the growth and popularity of triathlon (swimming, cycling and running) and the sport's welcoming of all ages has gone a long way to making this a viable alternative to running every day. Cycling does not have the jarring of running, while swimming is predominantly

The honourable Sir Rocco Forte, who at 60 plus takes part in marathons and triathlons, shows that age is no barrier.

Age is no barrier with the appropriate training.

Cycling can be an effective substitute for the pounding of running for the older athlete.

an upper body exercise and is a good balancing act for overall training. Both swimming and cycling are excellent forms of cardiovascular exercise.

Injuries

Frequent injuries can occur during running training (see Chapter 16) and running can be particularly wearing on the ankles, knees and hips of runners. Writing as an (ex/resting) runner who is waiting for both knees to be replaced, I certainly don't regret the miles and the hurt and the pain of my training years, I absolutely loved it. But, if I were to start again, I would certainly take more care to use stretching and mobility, strengthening of supplementary and complementary muscles, massage and recovery much more comprehensively. Runners who continue to run into old age are those runners who manage to avoid serious injuries. Some avoidance may be due to genetic inheritance and body make-up and shape, but a lot of injury avoidance will be down to how much care you take of yourself. It becomes more and more important to listen to your body; take notice of any aches and pains, and treat them all as potentially serious. You will not become unfit if you miss one day's training, on the contrary you will lengthen your ability to keep on running.

Women Runners

History

It should be remembered that it is only in the last 50 years that women have been allowed to race more than 800m, when the Rome Olympic Games of 1960 reintroduced the two-lap race, thus reversing the decision taken after the 1928 Olympic Games, when some poorly prepared women athletes collapsed at the end of the 800m. After 1960, the distances that women were allowed to run gradually increased, but it wasn't until 1972 that women were officially allowed to enter both the Boston and New York Marathons. The years leading to this had some amazing incidents.

In 1963 Merry Lepper (USA) finished the Culver City Marathon only after punching an official who attempted to drag her off the road.

In 1967 at the Boston Marathon, Kathrine Switzer disguised herself as a man (and wore a hood over her face!) to start the race. As with Lepper, officials tried to pull her off the course but were seen off when

Swimming is another good aerobic exercise to consider.

Top-class women's times are around 10 per cent slower than men's.

were allowed to enter but had to start 10min before the men – the women runners sat down and waited for the men's race to start.

In 1984 at the Los Angeles Olympic Games, women were finally allowed their Olympic Marathon. Since then the standard has risen dramatically with, currently, Paula Radcliffe (GB) holding the world record of 2h 15min 25sec, compared with Haile Gebrselassie's 2.3.59. (This seems to bear out one theory that women's times are approximately 10 per cent slower than men's.)

Comparison Times

There are exceptional female runners; however, the time difference percentage does seem to remain at about 10 per cent (this also applies to shorter distances). In comparison with another endurance sport, Ironman Distance Triathlon, Chrissie Wellington (GB) has the world record of 8.18.13 compared to Luc Van Lierde (Belgium) with 7.50.27, a percentage difference of less than 5 per cent. However, Van Lierde's record has lasted ten years, Wellington's was set in 2010. I would hazard a guess that the men's Ironman Triathlon world record is due for a change. (Since writing this chapter the men's Ironman world record has been lowered to 7.45.59 by Belgium's Marino Vanhoenacker on 3 July 2011 at Klagenfurt, Austria, and then just one week later down to 7.41.33 by Germany's Andreas Raelart in Roth, Germany.)

Despite the outstanding female runners, it seems unlikely that women will ever run faster than men. This does not in any way indicate that some women will not run a lot faster than the majority of men; only that at any comparable standard: local, County and District, National, International and World levels, men will beat women. There are a number of anatomical and physiological reasons for this. Women carry more body fat and less lean muscle than men who have a similar body mass. Because of increased body fat, less muscle mass and less powerful muscles, women have lower VO_2max to carry the same weight and body mass as men. Indications

Kathrine's boyfriend forcibly blocked their way. Switzer finished the Boston Marathon but was disqualified for four 'reasons':

1   She was running further than women were allowed.
2   She had competed against men.
3   She had lied on her entry form.
4   She ran without a chaperone!

However, largely because of these and other similarly tough-minded women distance runners, things began to change. At the New York Marathon in 1972, women

Women's marathon running is now an accepted part of World Championships.

are that women's muscles are not as efficient at producing speed and power when they contract, in comparison to men. When comparing the percentage differences in times and performances (not only at the marathon distance but equally at all distances), it seems that women's muscles are less efficient by that 10–11 per cent

Menstruation

Some female athletes suffer from irregular periods (amenorrhea) during times of heavy training; some athletes stop menstruating altogether. This is caused by the added stress on the runner's body of heavy training and competition, and can be extremely worrying, particularly for younger runners (and their families) who may not have experienced this before. However, menstruation will return after heavy training is stopped. If this does not occur, it is likely that there are other reasons involved and runners should seek medical advice.

It should be stressed that irregular periods do not normally occur unless the training is extremely heavy. The majority of women runners will not have amenorrhea or cease menstruating completely.

Women runners should be aware though, that there are some serious risks and implications with persistent amenorrhea. Enough oestrogen is not produced by the body, which causes the bones to lose calcium. If too much calcium is lost, the bones will become weak and more likely to fracture. In the long term, women with persistent amenorrhea will be at risk of fractures in later life, as well as during their running career.

CHAPTER 15

COMPARISON TIMES FOR MARATHON AND HALF-MARATHON AND OTHER DISTANCES

It is rare that anybody would run a marathon or even a half-marathon as their first race. Therefore it is valuable to know what times might be aimed for with some knowledge of times for other race distances. Similarly, it can be useful to know the equivalent times between linear and metric distances, to make realistic comparisons. However, if comparative marathon times are to be attempted, the runner must ensure that s/he has done adequate training for the longer distances.

The various formulae below are about 90 per cent accurate. They break down and become less accurate with very fast or very slow runners (and if non-appropriate training has been done). The comparisons are based on reasonable standard male athletes, and the equivalent times and comparisons for women athletes are set out in brackets. Slower male athletes are advised to use the women's figures; faster female athletes should use the men's comparisons.

10km and Half-Marathon

For finding an estimated marathon time, two very common and much used comparisons are:

- 10km time × 5 – 10min.
- Half-marathon time doubled + 6½min.

A good 10,000m time has the closest correlation to a half-marathon time from all the track events.

5,000m times are very relevant to half- and full marathon.

It is important to realize that experienced runners will slow down less than novice runners as the racing distance goes up, therefore the minus 10min for 10km comparisons are likely to be minus 12 to 15min for élite runners, and minus 5 to 7min for novice runners.

With these two examples we can look at three standards of runner: beginner, mid-pack and élite.

10km Time × 5 – 10min

A new marathon runner capable of 50min for 10km could reasonably expect to finish the marathon in 4h, i.e. 5 × 50 = 250min, less 10min gives 240min, therefore 4.00, more likely 4.03 to 4.05.

A mid-pack runner capable of 40min for 10km could reasonably expect to finish the marathon in 3h 10min, i.e. 5 × 40 = 200min, less 10min gives 190min, therefore 3.10.

An élite runner capable of 30min for 10km could reasonably expect to finish the marathon in 2h 20min, i.e. 5 × 30 = 150min, less 10min gives 140min, therefore 2.20, more likely 2.15 to 2.18.

Half-Marathon Time Doubled + 6½min

As with the 10km/marathon-time differences, experienced marathon runners will slow down less than novice runners as the racing distance goes up, therefore the +6½min for half-marathon comparisons are likely to be 5 or 6min for élite runners, and 10min or more for inexperienced runners.

A new marathon runner who has run 2h 15min for a half-marathon could reasonably expect to finish the marathon in 4h 37min, i.e. 2 × 2.15 = 4h 30min, plus 6½min gives 4.37, more likely 4.40.

A mid-pack marathon runner who has run 1h 30min for a half-marathon could reasonably expect to run 3h 7min for a full marathon, i.e. 2 × 90min plus 6½min.

An élite marathon runner who has run near to 1h for a half-marathon could reasonably expect to finish the marathon in 2h 6min, i.e. 2 × 1h = 2h, plus 6½min gives 2.06.30, possibly 2.04. Haile Gebrselassie's times of 58.55 for the half-marathon and 2.03.59 for the marathon distance would seem to bear this out.

Shorter Distance Comparisons

With the example of Haile Gebrselassie's times above, it should also be pointed out that he was also extremely successful at distances from 1,500m and 5,000m before moving up distance to half- and full marathon. There is no substitute for speed for top-class half-marathon and marathon running, and to have some speed over the shorter distances will ensure that your marathon times are faster – with the correct training (see Chapter 7). With this in mind, some comparisons of times from shorter distances are entirely appropriate.

Although Gebrselassie's times are not an exact comparison from as short as 1 mile right up to marathon distance, they are near enough (adjusting for his status as the world's premier marathon runner) to show that, with the correct distance training, a fast runner over the shorter distances can convert that speed into fast marathon running.

If we look at an imaginary runner, capable of a good club time of 39min for 10km (and therefore about 3h 5min for a marathon), what would he be capable of in the marathon if he worked on speed, and continued his endurance training? In an early season time-trial, he runs 4min and

Even 1,500m running times can have an impact on full and half-marathon running.

HAILE GEBRSELASSIE'S TIMES AND COMPARISONS

1,500m	3:33.73
1 mile	3:52.39
3,000m	7:25.09
2 mile	8:01.08
5,000m	12:39.36
10,000m	26:22.75
10 km (road)	27:02
10 miles (road)	44:24
Half-marathon	58:55
Marathon World Record	2:03:59

FINDING BEST TIMES

Using the mile as a starting point:

1 To find your best ½-mile time; halve your mile time and deduct 11sec (for women athletes, deduct 13sec).
2 To find your best 400m; halve your 800m and deduct 5½sec (for women athletes, deduct 6½sec).
3 To find your 2-mile time; add 20sec to your mile time and double it (for women athletes, add 24sec). This formula is also appropriate for 1,500m to 3,000m conversion.
4 To find your 3-mile time; multiply your mile time by 3 and add 75sec (for women athletes, add 90sec).
5 To find your best 6-mile time; double your 3-mile time and add 75sec (for women athletes, add 90sec). This formula is also appropriate for 5km to 10km conversion.

As with the conversions from 10km distance and half-marathon distance above, exact times will depend on fitness and experience of the runners. Conversion from 3 miles to 6 miles or 5km to 10km will be inaccurate if endurance training is insufficient.

The Kenyans and the Ethiopians, particularly Haile Gebrselassie (shown right here), have rewritten the record books for all distance running.

LINEAR TO METRIC

It is also necessary to be able to convert linear distances (miles and yards) into metric distances (kilometres and metres) and vice versa.

880yd to 800m	deduct 0.7sec.
1 mile to 1,500m	deduct 18 sec (men), 20sec (women).
2 miles to 3,000m	deduct 40 sec (men), 50sec (women).
3 miles to 5,000m	add 40 sec (men), 50sec (women).
5.6 miles to 10,000m	add 75 sec (men), 90sec (women).

40sec for a mile. By following our conversion formula:

- 4.40 mile = 15.15 for 3 miles (× 3 + 75).
- 15.15 for 3 miles = 31.45 for 6 miles (× 2 + 75).
- 31.45 for 6 miles = 33.00 for 10,000m (+ 75).
- 33.00 for 10,000m = 2.35 for a marathon.

An improvement of half an hour for the marathon distance.

All of these comparisons assume that you have done the correct, appropriate training for the marathon distance. Running a fast mile does not mean that you can go out and run a fast marathon!

There is one mathematical formula that is often used, although I am not convinced of its accuracy as it indicates that a runner capable of running a mile in 6min can run a marathon in 2h 45min (I think that

would be extremely difficult and unlikely) and also that a 4min miler would be way under 2h for the marathon. Given that Haile Gebrselassie's world record was a fraction under 2h 4min and that he has run a mile in 3.52, this seems to indicate that the formula may be better suited for comparisons between 5km, 10km and half-marathon.

The formula is:

$$T2 = T1 \times (D2/D1)1.06,$$

sometimes written as:

$$T2 = 1.06 \times T1 \times D2/D1,$$

where T1 is the given time, D1 is the given distance, D2 is the distance to predict a time for, and T2 is the calculated time for D2. It does seem to give much greater accuracy when comparing distances close to each other, e.g. 10,000m and half-marathon, 5,000m and 10,000m.

Importantly, knowing these comparisons means that drawing up your own training programme becomes easier (see Chapter 7).

CHAPTER 16

INJURIES AND THEIR PREVENTION

All runners should have an idea of the simpler and more common sports injuries and activity-related conditions, first-aid, self-help treatment and personal rehabilitation. The more serious conditions, such as fractures, dislocations, head, neck and back injuries, are not covered. Immediate medical attention should be sought. In the case of fractures, a knowledgeable first-aider can perhaps splint and immobilize the broken bone before the casualty is removed to hospital.

With head injuries, medical attention should be sought, and if any accompanying neck injury is suspected, the patient should not be moved. For any neck or spinal injury the patient should not be moved at all except by qualified medical or paramedical personnel.

Many runners are reluctant to visit a physiotherapist because of the cost of

treatment and consultation. However, qualified and expert advice is usually worth paying for in the long run, and a good physiotherapist will not impose a long and costly course of treatment if the patient can treat the injury him/herself. Advice can be given to the patient on correct self-help and rehabilitation.

What is a Running Injury and Why Correct Treatment is Important

Sprains, strains, contusions and fractures occur in situations when stresses like running are regularly imposed on the body.

The runner is usually anxious to return to running as soon as possible but problems occur when a return is attempted

before full healing has taken place and without proper rehabilitation. Problems can also occur when a lack of understanding of the injury results in improper treatment and rehabilitation, healing is incomplete and complications may develop. Lack of understanding of an injury can also cause anxiety.

The majority of the more common running injuries occur to the lower part of the body. Therefore feet, ankles, legs, knees, thighs, hips and the lower back, are particularly vulnerable.

Categorizing Running Injuries

Running injuries fall basically into two categories: traumatic and over-use.

Traumatic injuries occur suddenly and will be instantly obvious, although the full extent of the injury may not be obvious until investigation and examination have taken place by a qualified person. Such injuries usually occur as a result of a sudden twisting, over-stretching or collision, and will include joint sprains, dislocations, muscle strains, tendon strains, contusions (bruises) and bone fractures.

Over-use injuries occur gradually over a period of time and are often caused by repetitive actions, where incorrect bio-mechanics exist, or by too-rapid progression in training or by excessive competition, incomplete recovery and over-training.

Injuries may also be acute or chronic. **Acute** is when the injury has recently happened, within the first 24 to 48h. This is when first aid should be carried out aimed at reducing internal bleeding, swelling and inflammation.

An injury may sometimes occur just by falling during the race.

AIMS OF TREATMENT AND REHABILITATION

Short term:

- Prevent further damage.
- Limit bleeding.
- Reduce pain.
- Reduce swelling.
- Reduce inflammation.
- Prevent stiffness.
- Maintain muscle strength.

Long term:

- Prevent complications.
- Encourage full healing.
- Re-educate movement.
- Increase mobility.
- Increase muscle strength.
- Restore function for activity.
- Restore confidence in the injured part.
- Prevention of return of swelling.
- Prevention of re-occurrence.

Just the sheer physical impact of jarring during a distance race takes its toll.

Chronic injuries are those that have developed complications because of incorrect treatment, lack of treatment, poor rehabilitation or return to activity before full fitness of the injured part.

INFLAMMATION

- Tendonitis is inflammation of a tendon.
- Tenosynovitis is inflammation of a tendon sheath.
- Peritendonitis is inflammation of the soft tissues around the tendon (and thus is very similar to tendonitis and tenosynovitis).
- Bursitis is inflammation of a bursa (a bursa is a small fluid-filled sac, often found near joints, or where tendons pass over a joint, to prevent friction).

Sprains and Strains

Two common injuries are sprains and strains, they can often be confused:

- Sprains are injuries to joints.
- Strains are injuries to muscles and tendons and usually involve a tearing of fibres (e.g. a strained calf muscle; a strained Achilles tendon; a pulled hamstring. A 'pulled' muscle is the same as a strained or 'torn' muscle).

Grades or Degrees of Sprains and Strains

Joint Sprains

- Grade 1: Minimal damage; some loss of function.

- Grade 2: More ligament fibres damaged; partial detachment; degree of instability; swelling.
- Grade 3: Complete rupture; completely unstable; swelling.

Muscle Strains

- Grade 1: Small number of muscle fibres torn; fascia intact (fascia is the very thin connective tissue that binds and encapsulates muscle, muscle fibres and myofibrils); minimal bleeding.
- Grade 2: Larger number of muscle fibres torn; fascia intact; considerable bleeding which can be felt as mass. (If bleeding heals as a lump, it becomes an intra-muscular haematoma.)
- Grade 3: Large number of muscle fibres torn; fascia torn; bleeding diffuses and fills tissue spaces; intermuscular haematoma.
- Grade 4: Complete rupture of muscle; gap can be felt between two ends.

Intra-muscular haematoma: Muscle sheath intact; blood is contained within the muscle; haematoma forms within two hours.
Inter-muscular haematoma: Muscle sheath torn; blood seeps between muscles; blood tracks with gravity.

Soft-Tissue Injuries

All sports injuries, whether traumatic or over-use, involve damage to soft tissue. Soft-tissue includes muscle, tendon, ligament, synovial membrane, tendon sheath, skin, blood vessels and so on.

Soft-tissue injuries will result from contact (bruising), twisting and stressing joints (sprains), over-stretching muscles or tendons (strains), chafing and rubbing (local inflammation), fatigue and excessive action (over-use strains).

They can involve conditions such as torn fibres in muscles and tendons, torn and inflamed ligaments, inflamed tendons, inflamed tendon sheaths, inflammation of other connective tissue around tendon sheaths, inflamed joints and damaged joint capsule.

Inflammation is the body's reaction to injury or irritation. It involves local heat, pain, redness, swelling. Some or all of these symptoms may be present.

Treatment of Soft-Tissue Injuries:

All traumatic soft-tissue injuries will involve some degree of pain, inflammation, internal bleeding and swelling. Acute over-use soft-tissue conditions will involve pain, inflammation, possibly some internal bleeding, and swelling.

Immediate first-aid treatment is concerned with controlling inflammation, internal bleeding and swelling, thus alleviating pain to some degree and promoting faster healing, reducing the likelihood of

---

TREATING SOFT-TISSUE INJURIES

Immediate first-aid treatment of a soft-tissue injury involves RICE:

- **R**est.
- **I**ce.
- **C**ompression.
- **E**levation.

---

complications, and making physiotherapy treatment more effective.

Rest

Rest may be immediately obvious or even inevitable as sudden pain, pain on attempted movement, fear of further damage, and swelling will probably prevent movement. A longer period of rest is required in order to allow damaged tissue to start healing. This period of rest will vary according to the severity of the injury and may be a few days or more than a week. Rest may mean complete immobilization, abstention from attempted use and weight-bearing, or, after a period of initial healing time, may be 'active' rest where functional movement may not yet be possible, though gentle movements may be beneficial.

Ice

Ice should be applied to the injured part as soon as possible. The ice should be in a polythene bag (to stop leakage) and then applied to the body with a towel or other material against the skin to prevent ice burn. A bag of frozen peas or beans could be used as it will mould to the shape of an injured joint or other body part. Ice should be applied for about ten minutes, but should not be applied again within an hour. Ice should be applied regularly, at least for the first few days.

The physiological effects of ice treatment are:

1   Reduces pain: by reducing conductivity of nerve fibres.
2   Reduces stiffness: spasm is a natural reaction to pain, so by reducing pain, ice reduces spasm.
3   Reduces swelling: the initial response of the tissue is vasoconstriction, which limits the flow of blood. Use ice for approximately ten minutres for inflammatory conditions and the acute stage of injury to reduce bleeding and swelling.
4   Promotes repair: after the initial response of vasoconstriction, there follows vasodilation, which increases blood flow to help repair and healing. Use ice for about twenty minutes after the acute stage of injury to promote healing.

Do not apply heat during the acute stage of a soft-tissue injury. Heat will encourage internal bleeding and will aggravate the condition and increase inflammation.

Compression

Compression in the form of an elasticated bandage will help control the swelling. Swelling is initially not a bad thing. It is the body's natural 'splinting' or safety mechanism, which prevents further damage to an injured part by immobilizing it. But the body tends to over-compensate and swelling may be excessive causing pressure, pain and discomfort. Also, swelling will be increased by internal bleeding. Ice and compression are intended to reduce swelling and control it to a minimum. Excess swelling can hinder the healing process and lead to complications, or may interfere with an early diagnosis. The swelling is caused by an effusion of fluid into the inter-cellular spaces or between muscles, or between skin and bone, and is known as 'oedema'. Oedema differs from normal tissue fluid in that it contains plasma proteins and fibrinogen, a substance that causes blood to clot. It is a viscous fluid that can become more viscous (sticky) and adhesions can then occur; tissues that would normally slide smoothly over each

Basic rehabilitation and initial treatment of injury – RICE.

other become stuck together. Controlling the swelling by ice, compression and elevation, and later by gentle movement, can help prevent the formation of adhesions.

Elevation

Elevation helps control the swelling because fluids naturally flow downwards with gravity. Raising the injured part will help drain the oedema and reduce pressure and discomfort.

Acute Oedema

Swelling during the acute stage of an injury will consist of acute oedema. It is the acute oedema that we try to control and reduce with RICE treatment. Acute oedema will be soft, puffy, and painful.

Chronic Oedema

Chronic oedema will form if it is not controlled and reduced during the acute stage. Chronic oedema is then difficult to disperse and will require much massaging and friction to break down adhesions. Chronic oedema is tense, hard and the skin may be shiny.

Rehabilitation

Joints

As soon as possible after injury, and after a short period of healing has taken place, joints thrive on movement. This may be in the form of passive movement, where another person moves the joint through its range, then assisted active, and gentle active movement by the patient.

Movement for an injured joint during the rehabilitation stage acts as a form of natural massage and helps to disperse oedema, reducing swelling. It lubricates the joint by stimulating the secretion of synovial fluid and helps keep the muscles affecting the joint relaxed and toned.

All remedial movements of an injured joint should be carried out within the limits of pain (the exception might be with a true 'frozen shoulder' where the joint capsule has shrunk and requires stretching to prevent further shortening and a

chronic or permanent condition, but this will require a qualified diagnosis).

Muscles and Tendons

Injury to a muscle or tendon will heal better if the muscle is gently stretched as soon as possible after an initial period of healing. Scar tissue forms and is laid down during the healing process. Gentle stretching, fairly soon after the injury, will help the scar tissue to form long and not tight, and neatly in the direction of the muscle or tendon fibres. Without movement, the scar tissue can be laid down in an irregular fashion and can develop short, resulting in possible future tension in the muscle. Movement also helps to relax, tone and strengthen the muscle.

When soft tissue is damaged, scar tissue is formed. Scar tissue will contract by about the third week after injury and can continue to contract for up to seven months. It is, therefore, vital to gently stretch the new scar tissue while it is being laid down, as soon as possible after the acute injury stage has passed (approximately 48h), and it is vital to stretch the scar tissue regularly for at least seven months (a serious runner will include stretching as a regular routine).

Inflammatory Conditions

Inflammatory conditions such as tendonitis, tenosynovitis, bursitis, epicondylitis do not require movement. Such conditions often take a long time to recover and require complete rest. Movement is contra-indicatory. A doctor may prescribe anti-inflammatory drugs and/or cream or gel, but the patient must be disciplined enough to rest the inflamed part until complete recovery is achieved.

The Use of Heat During the Rehabilitation of Soft-Tissue Injuries

As previously stated, heat should not be used during the acute stage of a soft-tissue

---

PHYSIOLOGICAL EFFECTS OF HEAT IN INJURY TREATMENT

1 Vasodilation (promotes blood flow to the affected area).
2 Affects the sensory nerve endings (reduces pain).
3 Muscle relaxation.

Heat can also help when the whole body is subjected to it, e.g. a sauna bath:

1 Increases tissue metabolism.
2 Muscle relaxation.
3 Fall in blood pressure.
4 Increased activity of sweat glands.
5 General relaxation of mind and body.

---

injury (i.e. within the first 48h) as it will increase bleeding and encourage swelling. However, after the acute stage, when internal bleeding has stopped, heat can be very beneficial in aiding the healing process, relieving pain and relaxing muscles. Heat can be applied in a variety of ways: a hot-water bottle over the site of injury can be applied or hot, damp towels can be effective.

The easiest and most effective application of heat is an infra-red lamp. It should be positioned approximately 18 to 20in away from the skin surface at right angles above the injury.

Common Running Injuries and Conditions

Working upwards from the feet.

Foot

Pain across the 'ball' of the foot (the fore foot, where the toes meet the foot proper) is referred to as metatarsalgia. The pain is felt over the underside of the metatarsal heads, the ends of the bones of the spread of the foot, near their articulation (joint) with the bones of the toes (phalanges). This condition can occur occasionally in runners because of

Inevitably the feet take a pounding during a long race.

repeated impact on that part of the foot, or by a sudden increase in running mileage, by improper footwear or a combination of these factors.

The application of ice will help reduce inflammation and pain, but rest from the causative activity is essential for a while. Foot exercises can help mobilize the joints and strengthen the muscles of the foot, improving the arches. In persistent cases orthotics may help and the foot and running action may require examination by a podiatrician.

Arch Strain

Pain may be felt along the medial underside of the foot along the longitudinal arch. Strain occurs in this area because of a sudden increase in activity, repetitive impact or unaccustomed activity. The pain will be felt on walking and swelling may be apparent.

With rest, the condition should subside in about a week, but it can be helped by the application of ice or heat, and massage is often very soothing and beneficial.

Plantar Fasciitis

Pain is felt on the underside of the foot, towards the heel, and may feel as if there

is a small stone in the shoe at that point. The plantar fascia is a strip of connective tissue on the underside of the foot joining the middle three metatarsal bones to the heel bone (calcaneus), and it is at its attachment to the heel bone where inflammation develops.

Causes may include an increase in running mileage, or a sudden change in training, which stretches the underside of the foot.

Initial treatment may involve the application of ice over the inflamed area on the underside of the heel. Arch supports should help, and a soft pad to cushion the sore heel. Physiotherapy advice is extremely useful here, as this condition can become chronic if not treated properly and will result in a lot of pain.

Athlete's Foot

Athlete's foot is a fungal infection of the skin on the feet. It can occur anywhere on the foot, but is most common between the toes. It is an infectious condition that can be spread from one person to another through contact with floors, or can be spread from one foot to the other by mixing unclean socks.

The condition causes itching, and can become painful. The skin usually appears

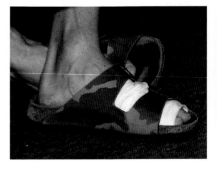

Strapping and bandages on cuts and injuries sustained during the race.

white, moist and soggy, especially between the toes. Similar fungal conditions around the rest of the foot may result in dry, flaky skin, which cracks and becomes sore. The condition is simple to treat with any of the variety of anti-fungal foot lotions.

Verruca

A verruca is an in-growing wart, usually found on the underside of the foot. It is caused by a virus and again can be spread from one person to another by barefoot contact with floors, or from foot to foot by interchanging of infected socks. In the early stages, a verruca appears as a small black spot. If untreated and allowed to develop it can enlarge and swell and may appear like a small volcano crater. At this stage it will be painful to walk on and may be painful if pressure is applied to the sides. Treatment is with a verruca medication, which contains salicylic acid.

Sprained Ankle

A sprained ankle is perhaps one of the most common injuries, and the most common type of ankle sprain is an inversion sprain, where the runner 'goes over' on the ankle, the weight going over the outside of the ankle, turning the foot inwards. This will damage the lateral ligament that holds the joint firm on the outside.

Immediate treatment is RICE. With a severe ankle sprain, a hospital check should be carried out, which will probably involve an X-ray in case of a fracture.

Other types of ankle sprain can occur, though are less common. The ankle may twist outwards with the body weight going on the inner edge, but this can often be accompanied by damage to the inner (medial) aspect of the knee joint. The ankle may be forced upwards (dorsiflexion) or downwards (plantarflexion).

In all cases, the immediate treatment is the same – RICE.

Rehabilitation

With an ankle sprain, a short period of immobilization will be inevitable during the acute stage and until bleeding and inflammation subside (approximately 48h). During this time, ice should be applied regularly for ten-minute periods. After 48h, ice may be used for longer periods of time.

Within the limits of pain, non-weight-bearing movement of the ankle should be attempted in an up and down direction. To regain some strength, isometric exercises (muscle tension without joint movement) should be carried out as soon as possible. While sitting, with the feet on the floor, press the toes down against the floor working the calf muscles and posterior tibial muscles at the back of the lower leg.

If one foot is placed on top of the injured foot, then the lower foot can be forced upwards against the resistance of the upper foot, thus working the anterior tibial muscles at the front of the lower leg.

Stretching exercises should be carried out as soon as possible, and while scar tissue is forming. Stretching reduces shortening of the scar tissue and adhesions, which cause complications. Stretching will involve gently turning the ankle in the direction that initially caused the injury, but this time in a very slow, controlled manner, and within the limits of pain. Body weight can be used to apply pressure, although in the early stages, passive stretching is advised. Stretching in all directions should be carried out to maintain flexibility in all the muscles that affect the joint.

Massage can be particularly beneficial, initially above the joint, massaging the calf region can help disperse oedema (swelling). During the rehabilitation phase, massage around the ankle, with 'frictions' (sideways or circling movements applied with pressure, moving the tissues below the surface) into the joint and over the site of injury and within the limits of bearable pain, can assist healing and reduce adhesions.

Specific strengthening exercises should be carried out as soon as possible. One-leg balancing, wobble-board balancing, calf raisers, dorsiflexion against a weight, can all be carried out before progressing to walking, running, hopping, sideways stepping and so on.

Calf Strain

Pain is felt in the calf region at the back of the lower leg, either in the belly of the muscle or at its junction with the Achilles tendon. Pain will be felt when using the muscle. Running should be avoided to prevent further damage. The muscle strain may be sudden (traumatic) or may develop gradually over a period of time (over-use), or as a result of an increase in training and a build-up of fatigue.

Immediate treatment is RICE then stretching exercises. Passive stretching

of the calf by dorsiflexing the foot and holding for about 10sec, or standing facing a wall and leaning into the wall with both legs straight and heels down to the floor. This can be progressed by having one leg back and one forward, pressing against the wall and slowly and gently forcing the back heel down to the floor. Hold the stretch position for 10sec or more. The stretch should be reasonably comfortable, not painful. As soon as possible, strengthening exercises such as calf-raises, should be carried out before starting walking and running.

Achilles Tendonitis/Strain

This condition can occur suddenly or gradually. If suddenly, some tearing of the tendon fibres has probably taken place with the resulting pain of inflammation. The condition may occur because of friction where the heel tab on the running shoe has rubbed and caused inflammation.

Achilles tendonitis can become chronic if not treated properly, and initial treatment will involve both rest and ice treatment, and stretching during healing. Ice should be applied for ten-minute periods regularly to reduce the inflammation. Rest is essential. Depending on the severity, running may not be resumed for up to six weeks. Complications occur when the runner tries to 'come back' too soon.

Deep-friction massage over the damaged spot will help break down any adhesions, but this should be carried out with professional advice before beginning stretching.

If peritendonitis/tenosynovitis develops and adhesions occur between the tendon and the tendon sheath, surgery may be the last resort.

Shin Splints

The term 'shin splints' is used as an 'umbrella' term to describe the pain felt along the inner or outer edge of the shin at the front of the lower leg. The pain may result from several causes:

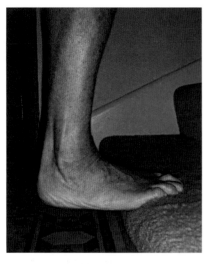 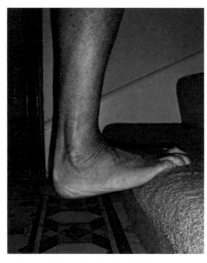 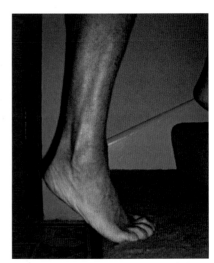

Self-help Achilles rehabilitation. FROM LEFT TO RIGHT: *starting position; heel lowered; heel raised.*

SIX-WEEK PROGRAMME FOR SELF-HELP AND REHABILITIATION FOR ACHILLES PROBLEMS

This example uses the right leg.
Work on this programme by combining it with as much cross-friction as you can bear, at least twice a day. It is much better to get someone else to do it to you, as they will give you more pain than you would stand yourself.

1 Both feet together with toes over edge of step or stair. Slowly lower heels until they are as stretched as possible (calves won't allow feet to drop any further). Lift up and extend on to toes. Do this 10 times, 3 times a day for one week.

2 Right foot with toes over edge of step or stair. Slowly lower heel until it is as stretched as possible (calf won't allow feet to drop any further). Lift up and extend on to toes. Repeat with left foot. Do this 10 times, 3 times a day for one week.

3 Back to both feet together with toes over edge of step or stair. Slowly lower heels until they are as stretched as possible (calves won't allow feet to drop any further). Then quickly rise on to toes. Do this 10 times, 3 times a day for one week.

4 Again, both feet together with toes over edge of step or stair. Quickly drop heels until they are as stretched as possible (calves won't allow feet to drop any further). Then immediately and quickly rise on to toes. Do this 10 times, 3 times a day for one week.

5 Right foot with toes over edge of step or stair. Slowly lower heel until it is as stretched as possible (calf won't allow foot to drop any further). Then quickly rise on to toes. Repeat with left foot. Do this 10 times, 3 times a day for one week.

6 Right foot with toes over edge of step or stair. Quickly drop heel until it is as stretched as possible (calf won't allow foot to drop any further). Then immediately and quickly rise on to toes. Repeat with left foot. Do this 10 times, 3 times a day for one week.

- Strain of the anterior tibial muscle on the outer side of the shin.
- Strain of the posterior tibial muscle behind the tibia can cause pain that can be felt along the shin bone.
- Anterior tibial compartment syndrome will cause pain on the outer side of the shin: with this condition, the anterior tibial muscle swells with exercise and becomes too big for its comparatively inelastic containing sheath.
- Posterior compartment syndrome: very similar to the above condition, but occurring in the muscles immediately behind the tibia (shin bone). Pain is felt along the inner edge of the shin bone.
- True shin splints: the pulling away of fibres and inflammation at the muscle attachment point on the shin bone. Pain may be felt along the inner edge of the shin (periostitis). Immediate rest is required and the condition may then heal in about two weeks.
- Stress fracture of the tibia.

All except the last condition can be brought about by repeated high impact activities, such as incorrect foot-plant, sudden change or increase in training, sudden increase in mileage when running.

For the last condition, immediate first-aid RICE treatment is required. Then get medical advice so that an accurate diagnosis can be obtained and treatment carried out.

Knee

The knee is a particularly vulnerable joint with runners as it has to withstand a lot of

Shin strapping.

pressure and stress. It is a very strong joint, gaining stability from the very strong joint capsule, specific ligaments and powerful muscles of the thigh. However, with the excesses of stress to which it is subjected in distance running, and in some cases mistreatment or neglect by the runner, it can be easily damaged. The knee is basically a hinge joint, but is more complex as there is some rotation possible, particularly when bent. If bent during extreme load bearing, sprain and dislocation can occur. This can

Unwrapping strapping that needed to be applied before the event.

result in damage to specific ligaments at the sides of the joint, or which cross within the joint, and damage to the joint capsule and synovial membrane, as well as possible damage to the semi-lunar cartilages. When the joint is locked out, the lower leg rotates slightly outwards. If locking out occurs under weight-bearing pressure then there is the possibility of damage to the semi-lunar cartilages within the joint.

Also forming part of the knee joint is the knee cap (patella), which is a sesamoid bone that forms within the quadriceps tendon and acts as a pivot for the very strong tendon that crosses the joint. The patella articulates on its underside with the front lower end of the femur, and can suffer injury, inflammation and wear and tear degeneration as a result of impact, over-use, misuse and neglect.

The knee joint has many bursae (small fluid-filled sacs which prevent friction where tissues have to pass over bony surfaces) that can become inflamed with over-use and misuse.

Because the knee is such a complex joint, pain can vary from general pain

around the joint to pain felt over numerous specific sites. It is best to get medical and physiotherapy advice. However, there are some common injuries that can be identified and treated.

Twisted Knee (Sprain)

Runners can suddenly twist their knee joint. The joint is wrenched because of excess force, either by contact or in weight-bearing during movement. Damage is likely to occur to the ligament on the inner side of the joint (medial ligament), and to the ligament on the outer side of the joint (lateral ligament). There is the possibility of damage to the two cruciate ligaments, which cross over inside the joint, and it is possible that damage will occur to the joint capsule and synovial membrane. The joint will be painful and may feel insecure. If the ligaments are damaged, the joint will be insecure and no further weight-bearing movement should be attempted.

As always, the initial first-aid treatment is RICE. Depending on the severity of the sprain, the runner is likely to be out of action between two weeks and three months. However, as soon as possible after the acute stage (48h), passive movement and gentle non-weight-bearing movement should be attempted. This will act as a natural massage to help disperse the swelling and will also help to maintain some tone in the muscles. It is particularly important to try to maintain some tone and strength in the quadriceps muscles of the front of the thigh, as these muscles play a strong part in the stability of the knee joint, and can be very quick to atrophy (waste). Straight leg exercises can be carried out almost straight away, within the limits of pain, where the straight leg is lifted, and making sure the knee is straightened completely.

Cartilage Damage

Cartilage damage can occur as a complication with a knee sprain. It may not be obvious at the time and may manifest itself later, as the patient still has pain during the rehabilitation stage. However, it is possible that cartilage damage is obvious at the time of injury with sharp pain and difficulty in fully straightening the knee. The likelihood is that a piece of dislodged cartilage is interfering with the normal joint movement.

Start with normal self-help (RICE), but then medical advice is essential as the only treatment for damaged cartilage is specialized physiotherapy or surgery.

Iliotibial Tract Syndrome

This is a common over-use condition particularly contracted through running. The iliotibial tract is a band of fascia (very strong, very thin connective tissue) connecting the gluteal muscles and the muscles of the thigh to the tibia below the knee joint, and as such must pass over the knee joint. During the repetitive action of running, this band of tissue is moving to and fro across the side of the joint and can become inflamed. Pain is felt on the outer side of the knee. The pain may become more severe while running so that running has to stop. First-aid treatment involves the application of ice for ten minutes over the painful spot, and the runner must rest from running.

It is possible to stretch the outer thigh and gluteal region by crossing the injured leg over the other and pulling the foot upwards along the outer side of the lower leg although there is considerable discussion about the effectiveness of this.

Chondromalacia Patella

Another over-use condition, particularly common through running, that is more of a simple mechanical fault condition rather than a proper over-use injury, brought about by an imbalance in strengths of the muscles which make up the quadriceps group.

Pain is felt in/below the knee cap (patella). The pain may be felt specifically on the lower part of the front of the knee cap, and also around the sides of the knee cap, particularly when going up or down stairs, or when running downhill. It may also hurt when standing up after sitting down for some time. The pain results from inflammation on the underside of the patella where it articulates with the femur. It is particularly common in young girls and women because of the greater angle of

the femur on the tibia as a result of the wider pelvis.

In older runners there may be some temporary inflammation, but it is also quite likely that wear-and-tear degeneration has taken place. The cause of this degeneration is a loss of strength in the vastus medialis muscle in the quadriceps (the inner of the four quadriceps muscles) in comparison to the strength in the other three muscles.

A common cause is running with poor technique. First-aid treatment may involve the application of ice to reduce pain, but full treatment of the condition will involve correcting the situation that caused the weakening of the muscle, and then specifically strengthening up the vastus medialis muscle in the thigh.

This is done with plenty of straight-leg exercises:

(a) Sit on the floor with legs out straight, press the back of the knees down against the floor.
(b) Sit on the floor, legs out straight, lift one straight leg up at a time.
(c) As (b) above, but with a small weight attached to the foot.

The above exercises are obviously recommended as remedial exercises to try to correct the condition, but it is worthwhile carrying them out regularly as preventative exercises. Many sports injury doctors believe the majority of knee conditions involve some degree of chondromalacia patella, and recommend straight-leg exercises for remedial and preventative purposes.

Many runners instinctively put on a knee bandage (elastic tubular knee support) if they have any kind of knee pain. However, it is important that an elasticated knee-support is not worn in cases of chondromalacia patella because it presses the knee cap against the femur and aggravates the problem.

Leg press or leg-extension machines should not be used for remedial quad strengthening in a case of chondromalacia patella because the dynamic movement of the knee joint and the tension of the quadriceps through the quadriceps tendon

will again press the knee cap against the femur and aggravate the condition.

Thigh

Injuries can occur to the quadriceps muscles at the front of the thigh, or to the hamstring muscles at the back of the thigh. If a strain occurs to either the quadriceps or the hamstrings, then the initial first-aid and self-help treatment is RICE for the first 48h. Heat should not be applied in the early stages.

Muscle strains in the quadriceps or hamstrings can be traumatic (happening suddenly) because of strong, rapid stretching or contraction, or they may be over-use (occurring gradually with increasing severity) because of excessive work or fatigue.

Rehabilitation

After the initial 48h, by which time internal bleeding should have subsided because of correct RICE treatment, it is important to try to maintain flexibility by stretching the affected muscle(s). Stretching should be carried out to discomfort rather than pain. Stretching of the muscle during healing helps the healing of scar tissue. Rest from running may be necessary for a while. However, as soon as pain-free stretching of the muscles has been achieved, then specific strengthening exercises can be carried out.

Complications can develop, particularly with quadriceps strains. If there is a lot of internal bleeding, the blood may solidify and the formation of bone may then occur within the muscle (myositis ossificans). It is vital, therefore, that enough rest and treatment with ice is carried out in the early stages. No attempt should be made to massage the muscle too early and particularly if it is painful and where there is bruising.

Adductor Strain and Groin Strain

Strains to the adductor muscles are common in runners. Strain may occur in the belly of the muscle where fibres are torn, or pain and discomfort may be felt high up in the groin region around the tendonous attachment with the pelvis (groin strain.).

Adductor strain and groin strain may occur suddenly because of a dynamic, ballistic movement or by the leg slipping sideways on ice or muddy ground, or an over-use injury when a runner suddenly increases the amount of hill training. Injury may also occur because of a lack of flexibility in those muscles. However, pain in the groin may be a symptom of another condition such as an inguinal hernia, strain and inflammation of the inguinal ligament or pubic symphisis, or even referred pain from the back. As ever, if pain persists, get medical advice.

Treatment and Rehabilitation
This is a delicate area to apply ice. Although its application may assist with the healing of a minor over-use strain, ice may be essential in the initial treatment of a more severe strain. Rest from running is essential, but as soon as possible, gentle stretching should start. Stretches should include lunging sideways on the uninjured leg so that the 'injured' leg trails straight and to the side, thus stretching the inner thigh.

Another method is to sit on the floor with knees bent and to the side, with the soles of the feet together. Hold the ankles and gently press the elbows against the inside of the knees, which presses the knees outwards. Alternatively, if this sitting position is awkward, you can lie on your back with knees bent and falling to the side, with the soles of the feet together. Hands can be placed on the inside of the knees and gently push downwards and

outwards. With rest and gentle stretching, a groin strain should heal within one to two weeks.

To strengthen the adductor muscles after injury, and when pain has subsided, isometric exercises can be carried out. One method is to hold a ball between the feet or knees and squeeze the ball inwards. Other exercises include lying on the side, head resting in hand with elbow on the floor, the other hand on the floor in front of the body; cross the top leg over the lower straight leg and rest the foot on the floor in front; lift and return the lower straight leg for a number of repetitions.

Abdominal Muscles

Strain of the abdominal muscles is uncommon, although a minor strain can occur when runners carry out excessive abdominal strengthening exercises or are new to abdominal strengthening.

Usually a localized painful spot is felt in the abdominal region and pain will probably be felt when the muscles are contracted or stretched. Once again, as with any muscle strain, rest, and the application of ice should be carried out.

A minor strain should heal and be free from pain between one and two weeks and gentle stretching of the abdominal region should be started. The simplest method of stretching the abdominals is to lie face down on the floor, place hands on the floor underneath the shoulders, and lift up the trunk by straightening the arms. Do not force the trunk upwards excessively as this can place stress on the vertebrae

of the lower back. Lift to a comfortable stretch and then press the chest forward.

Once abdominal strengthening exercises are resumed, don't do them at too high an intensity. Do them comparatively slowly to avoid any ballistic stretching on the return from the curl. It is important to carry out abdominal strengthening exercises correctly and safely to protect the lower back. 'Abdominal curls' are much safer and more effective than 'sit-ups', as they do not involve the hip flexor muscles as prime movers. Also it is vital, with any abdominal curl exercises (or 'sit-ups'), that the knees are well bent and the feet flat on the floor.

Tenosynovitis

Tenosynovitis is inflammation of the synovial sheath (sometimes referred to as tendon sheath) that covers the tendon, the purpose of which is to allow smooth movement of the tendons beneath the connective binding tissues. The condition will have been caused by some change in activity; either a new activity or an increase in training or competition. Obviously it is important to try to identify the cause.

IMPORTANT

- Treat any injury as potentially serious.
- Do not expect injuries simply to disappear by themselves.

CHAPTER 17

THE DAY OF THE RACE

Why do you need to race? You don't – but having an aim, an objective is one of the most important ways to ensure that you maintain your training. Without a goal, all that training can sometimes seem to be pointless.

New athletes get nervous, and none more so than new marathon and half-marathon runners. Even with the popularity of half- and full marathon, it can still seem to be a daunting challenge with all the possible variables it has: weather, course, other competitors. If you are one of those people who get very nervous, one way of dealing with nerves is to anticipate after the race, rather than the race itself. What will you tell your friends? How will they react to you having completed your big challenge? How good will you feel about yourself when you've completed the event? These things are important and can be a big factor in ensuring that not only do you race, but that you race well.

Your first half- or full marathon is something special, it's something that sets you apart from the majority of the population. It is your chance to show how hard you've worked and what you've already achieved. Taking part and finishing your first half- and full marathon is one of those things that you will remember all your life. And there are so many things that we can do in the final few days and on race-day itself that will help you to your best possible race.

Before we look at all the positive things we can do to race well, let's take a look at things that can go wrong and how best to avoid them.

Many new distance runners continue to train too hard going into a race, you must avoid this (see Chapter 13). But there are other things as well: suffering from nerves (see Chapter 9), incorrect food, lack of sleep, travelling too close to the race, not knowing the course properly, not knowing your actual starting time, inappropriate kit and equipment

The preparation for your first race has really started the day you began training for the half- and full marathon; the final preparation begins a week before. For your race, you want to feel as good as you possibly can – fit, relaxed and confident. I would encourage you to make a timetable or time-line checklist and go through it step by step in the lead-up to your event. Following a timetable gives a sense of order to preparations and takes away a lot of nervousness.

The Weekend Prior to the Race

Do an early check on your race kit including numbers and pins. Check whether or not you will be wearing a transponder around your ankle and your travel arrangements.

If the race is a long way away, check that you have booked accommodation – telephone just to make sure that they have your reservation. Look up the maps and ensure that you know the directions and the likely time it will take. How will you get from the hotel to the race start?

The Day Before the Race

Ensure that you have all the necessary clothes and equipment packed. For immediately before the race, make sure that you have warm clothing, a water bottle to keep hydrated, an energy snack in case you have been too nervous to eat breakfast properly and your race details.

CHECKLIST

For the race itself you must have:

- running vest
- running shorts
- running shoes (how will you ensure that the laces don't come loose?)
- socks
- safety pins
- water bottle (discard at the start)
- Vaseline and/or talcum powder.

For after the race:

- tracksuit or warm clothes
- something to eat and drink.

The Afternoon and Evening Before the Race

Check out the race-information pack and go to the pre-race briefing. Particularly check what time your race starts. Is there a different start time for élite athletes to other runners? Is there more than one start? There are three different starting places for the London Marathon, coloured red, blue and green; make sure you know which starting colour/place is yours. Remember you alone will be responsible for getting to the correct start at the correct time. Most big races will have time indicators at the start so that you can 'seed' yourself into the appropriate slot. Don't be tempted to upgrade yourself to a faster anticipated time than you are capable of – you will end up going off too fast, being overtaken and feeling totally dispirited. If you do have any questions, don't be afraid to ask them but do check that they're not already answered in the race pack

Be prepared early.

— athletes hate hearing questions asked when a little bit of reading will have already answered them. Be sure that you know the course by reading the race-pack information and looking at the maps. If you have a chance and you get to the race venue early enough, it's worth driving around the course if it's accessible. It is worth asking if there are any unusual aspects of the course. Essentially, ensure that you know whether the course is open (normal traffic will be operating) or closed to traffic.

Take it easy, you'll feel nervous but tell yourself that it's a good nervousness. Have a meal but try not to have anything too heavy on the stomach. If you can, stay with your normal food as much as possible. There's no point in changing to a bowl of pasta the night before the race just because other people have advised it; stay with the food you know, any radical

adjustment will not do any good and may even be detrimental. If you do have to travel and stay overnight, be sure you can get something acceptable to eat. If in any doubt at all, take your own food.

Getting a good night's sleep may be unlikely whether you're at home or in a hotel but do try to rest. Lie around, watch television or listen to music. Many distance runners think that it's not the sleep the night before the event, but rather two nights before. You'll probably be at home then so a good sleep should be easier.

Make sure your water bottles are filled up, either with water or the drink supplement that you are used to. Never experiment with something new on race day. Put your race numbers on your race top. It's important that you don't cut or change the numbers in any way.

The Morning of the Race

Most races in Britain have fairly early morning starts, so a lie-in is highly unlikely. It really isn't worth working out just how long you dare to stay in bed, you'll probably be awake before the alarm goes anyway. Give yourself enough time to wake up properly and get to the race in adequate time. If you have to drive and park at the race venue, make sure you know where the race parking is and if there are any restrictions.

Eat breakfast. Even if you're nervous, you must have something. Again choose something familiar that you know won't upset your stomach. Drink, drink and drink again. Water is best but, contrary to

Enjoy the day.

Know where the toilets are located and also find out if there are any alternative toilets nearby.

Take as much time as you need to get into your starting spot. Use the timelines and displays, and ensure that you aren't rushing there just before the start and you can't get to where you want to be. Stand there and mentally visualize exactly what you will do and what routine you will follow. There won't be much space but that will be the same for everybody.

Are you the type of person who needs to be around the action? Or do you like calmness and quiet before a race? It's your choice and choose what is appropriate for you, not what everyone else appears to be doing. Again, focus on what you will do. Go through in your mind the start, the early pace, the mid-section, the latter stages when you're getting tired and fatigued, and the finish. Also think about how much training you've done – particularly think of all the things that you've given up so you've been able to train for this event

Make sure that you've had enough water, keep sipping from your water bottle.

Immediately Before the Start

Be in the starting line-up area in plenty of time. Check that you're where you should be, in the appropriate time zone. Stretch your shoulders and upper body, roll your neck to lose any tension. Make yourself mentally strong and positive about the race. First, try to relax (squeezing the shoulders and fists as tight as you can and then instantly relaxing can help), then imagine yourself doing well in the actual race.

After the Race

Enjoy the feeling – you're a marathon or half-marathon runner and a finisher! Nothing can take that away from you.

popular opinion, one cup or tea or coffee will not do you any harm.

You'll probably want to stretch, so decide if you want to do it at the race site or before you get there.

Even with perfect pre-race preparation, things have a habit of taking longer than you anticipate, so give yourself more time than you think you'll need. It's worth making out a timeline list for your first race and trying to stick to it. Don't forget the toilets! Race-venue toilets have a habit of being particularly busy before an event, there are a lot of nervous athletes around.

Anyone can race a marathon.

The spectators will help you through.

BE POSITIVE

Tell yourself:

- 'I'm really looking forward to this.'
- 'I have prepared extremely well and I'll be able to cope with the weather and course conditions.'
- 'I will finish this race.'
- 'I will race my own race and not let anyone or anything distract me.'

Drink some water immediately; eat something to get some energy back in your body, within 20min, if possible. Put on warm, dry clothing and walk easily for a few minutes (jogging may be a little difficult). If you can bear to stretch, do that as well, it will pay dividends for the following day.

Think back on what you've done, what you had to do in preparation for it.

Enter your next race!

Paula Craig racing in a wheelchair. Paula is the only athlete to have run and pushed the London Marathon.

CHAPTER 18

AFTER THE RACE

Whether it's your first marathon or half-marathon, or your 10th or your 50th, there is an amazing sense of achievement when you've crossed the finish line. Enjoy it! If it is your first experience of the full or half-marathon, then you've done something that very few people have done in their life. Having set the goal of finishing, having given up all those hours for training, having made major changes in your life in sleeping, leisure time, eating, drinking and, importantly, what you have sacrificed to do these things, will have had a profound effect on your life. The obstacles that you have overcome, including perhaps other people's prejudices and opinions, will

have made you a mentally much tougher person. So what now?

Let's deal with immediately after the race, that evening and night, and then the next day, week and month, before looking at long-term decisions.

Immediately After the Race

As soon as you can after finishing, drink and eat, then drink and eat some more. Replenish your water and energy systems. You may not feel like it, but it will pay dividends. Get warm clothing on; tired cold muscles will stiffen quickly and make recovery more difficult. If you can bear to, stretch, but stretch gently. You may feel even more aches as you do so, but tomorrow

(probably even in bed that night) you will feel better and more recovered.

The Evening After the Race

Sleeping after a big race is never easy. Many athletes and non-athletes think that the sheer tiredness and exhaustion after an endurance event will ensure a good night's sleep. The reverse is true; the adrenaline, the memories – good and bad, the aches and pains, and the reliving of the occasion will make a broken, restless sleep extremely likely. Don't worry, this happens to everybody, so just be prepared for it. Two nights afterwards you'll barely be able to wake up the next morning.

The Next Few Days

If you've always managed to walk up and down stairs, you're in for a big shock the next morning! Your leg muscles particularly, but also your back, shoulders, stomach and backside muscles will be tight and sore. This soreness is called delayed onset of muscle soreness (DOMS) and it is caused by the tough repetitive exercise from the marathon. Just the sheer jarring of the feet and legs hitting the ground for all those steps (experienced runners have calculated it can be around 60,000 steps for a marathon) will have exhausted you. Remember that the lifting and falling effect of the bodyweight while running means that between two and four times the bodyweight hits the ground on each running step – that is an immense amount of trauma to deal with. Again, stretching, massage and hydration, along with a steady refuelling of complex carbohydrates

After the race.

Hug after the race.

Rest – you've earned it.

It hurt, but it's over.

marathon race was at Wolverhampton many years ago, and I was running 10 miles within 4 days. Probably crazy, but true nonetheless. Do be aware that, even if you think you have completely recovered, it is likely that your body will need more time, and starting to train again too soon may well mean that proper recovery will take much longer and may increase the chances of picking up an injury. However, do run a little when you feel you can, as little as a 5min jog will actually help you to recover. Gradually build up the distance of your runs.

Rethink

Depending on your (first) marathon (or half) experience, there are one of two thoughts that entered your mind as you crossed the line, 'Never again!' or 'I can't wait to do another one!' depending on your level of soreness and pain in the days after; that first thought may well change. Some people are happy that they have completed one marathon or half-marathon, almost a box to tick and then to move on. For many of us, that first one just sows the seeds. The 'if' evaluation begins: if I ran more miles, if I had a coach, if I joined a running club, if I started to do some speed training; should I look at my running technique, where can

(see Chapter 10), are all essential to recover as quickly as possible. Experienced runners will often sit in a cold bath, or even an ice bath, to allow their legs to recover more quickly.

Gradually you will feel better, gradually the soreness will go away (experienced runners talk about how quick the recovery is when you have had a 'good' race compared to a disappointing one). You would imagine that a faster run would mean extra soreness; however, it appears that the euphoria of a great run means a faster recovery. I agree with this, my best

I get good advice, what race should I do next, should it be a half- or full marathon or something else?

Having started the running habit, I believe it is important to enter another race. It doesn't have to be a marathon or half-marathon, but there is a need to have an aim. If there isn't a goal to aim at, it can become dangerously easy to rationalize, 'Why am I doing this? Why am I training?' That future race becomes a major factor in helping you to remain fit, healthy, active and running. As with entering your first marathon or half-marathon, give yourself enough time to prepare properly. There are runners who will run full marathons frequently but they are unlikely to do themselves justice. If your marathon was one of the big city races, then perhaps look for an entirely different experience with one of the smaller, off-the-beaten-track marathons; and if your marathon was one of the smaller ones, then look to enter the London Marathon, or even one of the other majors: Chicago, Berlin, New York, Boston. Give yourself the incentive to carry on!

A space blanket for warmth immediately after finishing.

USEFUL INFORMATION

There are so many websites, books, magazine articles and so much information on marathon and half-marathon races, preparing and training for them, and just about anything remotely connected with them that it would be impossible to give anything but a brief introduction as to where and how to progress.

The following magazines and their associated websites will give you a wealth of information:

Runner's World, Running Fitness, Women's Running, Men's Running, Distance Running.

Athletics Weekly has a whole range of articles about running all distances.

Excellent websites, which will give you inside information on the 'big' races, include: www.worldmarathonmajors.com and www.london-marathon.co.uk

All the charities have websites and these are most easily accessed by Googling the London Marathon website, and the introduction page will give you the charities and how to enter the marathon through them.

All good running shops will normally have active runners working in them and will happily give you advice on preparation, kit and shoes. Central London has the London Marathon Store at 63 Long Acre, Covent Garden, London, WC2E 9JN.

It is very, very easy to get advice on all aspects of marathon and half-marathon running through the websites, magazines and shops.

Perhaps a marathon isn't long enough for you? And you progress to ultra-running or ultra-distance triathlon!

INDEX